Assessment Myths

Applying Second Language Research to Classroom Teaching

LIA PLAKANS
University of Iowa

ATTA GEBRIL
The American University of Cairo

Ann Arbor
University of Michigan Press

ISBN-13: 978-0-472-03581-6

2018   2017   2016   2015   4   3   2   1

Acknowledgments

This book is a result of our ongoing collaboration; however, others were instrumental in getting to a final product. We would like to thank Barbara Plakans, who has many years of experience in language testing, ESL, and editing. Her close reading and commenting on issues large and small helped us think through challenging chapters and clarify difficult concepts in language testing. Kelly Sippell, our editor, also guided us through with thoughtful comments and questions as well as with her support and belief in the project. We also thank several anonymous reviewers who offered their suggestions and advice at various stages in the process.

Atta would like to thank Professor Michael Eid of the Free University in Berlin (FUB) for hosting him during the summers 2013 and 2014. Atta's stay during this period instrumentally helped in finishing this book. Atta's thanks are extended to Angela-Beatrice Coenders who provided invaluable administrative support during his stay at FUB. A grant from the European Commission and a pre-tenure sabbatical from the American University in Cairo provided substantial support during the writing of this book.

Preface

Our experience with language assessment began as teachers—Lia in a community literacy/ESL program in Texas and Atta teaching EFL at a university in Egypt. Over the years, we have taught in many other contexts as well—Atta in U.S. Arabic language programs and Lia in intensive English programs in Ohio and Iowa. We met in graduate school at the University of Iowa where we both specialized in language assessment. Both of our dissertations compared integrated reading-writing assessment with independent writing assessment. Atta focused on the scores and reliability of the two test forms using advanced statistical analysis, while Lia considered what writers did as they composed the two kinds of tasks. Our shared interest in integrated assessment led to collaboration on several research projects over the years. Along with this research, we both continue to work with language teachers—Atta working with MA TESOL students at the American University in Cairo and Lia with Foreign Language and ESL teacher education and graduate students at the University of Iowa. These experiences have grounded our assessment work in research and also provided us with practical implications and applications for the classroom.

Writing this book together was a valuable experience. Sorting through the myths, the research, real-world examples, and applications illuminated the multiple voices and worldviews that exist in the field of language teaching and assessment. For this reason, some of the myths may not ring true for readers holding differing presumptions. Even between the two of us, at times we had to debate our beliefs as we developed these chapters. In the end, we wrote a book that represents our shared knowledge, understanding, and thoughts about language assessment and teaching. We hope, through this book, to offer teachers and students an understanding of the multifaceted discipline of language assessment.

Contents

Introduction

Testing in general strikes a deep emotional chord in people. Those who enjoy competition are up for the challenge, but most of us would rather forgo the ordeal. Language testing is particularly daunting because it does not just attempt to assess our knowledge about a specific subject but assesses how effectively, as test-takers, we are capable of communicating with the rest of the world.

At the same time that a test is making examinees fearful, teachers and test developers must worry about basic issues of fairness, utility, and the power tests hold over other people's futures. Sometimes high stakes are involved: passing a course, qualifying for study abroad, admission to a degree program, or having access to citizenship or employment. To sympathetic EFL/ESL teachers, anxious to see their students develop self-confidence and reluctant to crush their efforts, assessing their students' skills can be painful. They seek to empower and not judge.

With all of this emotion and trepidation stirred up by assessment and how it is performed, is it any wonder that myths should develop?

This book, *Assessment Myths: Applying Second Language Research to Classroom Teaching*, follows others in the University of Michigan Press series on myths in language learning and teaching. This volume has adopted the same framework as previous Myths books to illuminate important issues that impact language teaching and learning. Each chapter presents a myth, reviews research that qualifies or debates the myth, and concludes with suggestions for applying the research. It is our hope that this book will provide interesting conversations as well as valuable content for courses in language teaching and assessment.

How do we define language assessment? How did we decide which eight myths to include? What are some key terms in language assessment? These fundamental issues will be introduced first.

What Is Language Assessment?

In language learning, evaluation should be an integral part of the teachers' decision-making, their students' self-reflection, and the long-term instructional operations. Assessment takes different forms and serves many purposes in instructional contexts. These purposes can range from a student answering a teacher's question to an applicant taking an entrance exam. In addition, the uses of language assessment are broad and life-altering, from informing teaching to fulfilling citizenship requirements. Language teachers and programs use assessment to make many decisions—diagnostic, placement, exiting, and hiring, to name just a few.

Given their ubiquitous and powerful status, language assessments should be considered carefully and developed thoughtfully. We look to assessment to provide information about language abilities. This goal is often more complicated than it first appears. For example, interviewing language learners or asking them to write on a given topic provides a seemingly transparent picture of their ability to use language. However, their responses can be affected by many issues other than language such as the test-taker's familiarity with the topic, prior experience with tests, level of anxiety, and clarity of the instructions for the task. When assessing learners' listening skills, we cannot actually know what they comprehend without asking them to use other skills, such as reading test questions or writing a response. Despite or maybe because of these complications, the field of language assessment has grown over the years and continues to seek answers and best practices for these dilemmas. This book provides an overview of research, theory, and application on many of the issues in language testing.

Developing an assessment is difficult for the reasons just explained. Even a well-developed test can cause challenges for teachers if it does not measure the skills to be evaluated. The purpose of the test should be a primary concern in selecting what to use. For example, an end-of-term exam should be designed to include the skills and content covered in the course. If a test's design is not aligned with its purpose, then the test results may not be meaningful. Such misalignment is not uncommon and will be a recurring theme throughout this book because that alignment is the key to valid, ethical, and fair assessment. This issue is important in both large-scale standardized tests and classroom assessments. As teachers, we need to ask ourselves regularly, "Why am I giving this test?" and "What do I hope to learn about my students/class/teaching?" The answers to these questions should help identify useful tests and remind us that testing should be for learning and not for unknown or, even worse, punitive purposes.

Assessments come in many shapes and forms. Probably the first thing that comes to mind involves performances on tasks or questions to be answered in an allotted amount of time. Perhaps the most familiar form is a paper-based test that includes multiple choice, fill-in-the-blank, and/or sentence completion questions. More recently language testing has included performance-based assessments, such as participating in an interview or writing a short essay. In classroom assessment, the **process** can be evaluated along with the **product**; the preparation of portfolios requires students to first collect samples of their work over a period of time and then reflect on their choices. This depth of information about students' progress during the semester enlightens end-of-course decisions and helps with future placement. Each of these formats has advantages and shortcomings that should be considered when developing language assessments.

Why These Eight Myths?

The power that tests have in affecting people's lives is one likely reason for the many myths that exist about assessment. Test-takers and students create theories about how to get a high score, while teachers or administrators ponder how to interpret test scores. The nature of myths is that they are not entirely false. Anthropologists study myths in cultures because they reflect worldviews, values, and explanations for inexplicable phenomena. The assessment myths explored in this book also have reasons for existing and, in some cases, contain some element of truth. In each chapter we will dissect the myth to illuminate the complexities of the topic as well as what can make it problematic for classroom teachers.

As assessment specialists and long-time language teachers, we have encountered many myths, and at times have held some myths of our own. We used these experiences to select myths for this book. We narrowed our list to eight myths by asking ourselves three questions: (1) Does this myth address a critical issue in language assessment? (2) Are there theories and research that delve into the truth behind this myth? and (3) Is this myth important to teachers? The answers left us with these myths:

> **Myth 1: Assessment is just writing tests and using statistics.**
>
> **Myth 2: A comprehensive final exam is the best way to evaluate students.**
>
> **Myth 3: Scores on performance assessments are preferable because of their accuracy and authenticity.**
>
> **Myth 4: Multiple choice questions are inaccurate measures of language but are easy to write.**
>
> **Myth 5: We should test only one skill at a time.**
>
> **Myth 6: A test's validity can be determined by looking at it.**
>
> **Myth 7: Issues of fairness are not a concern with standardized testing.**
>
> **Myth 8: Teachers should not be involved in preparing students for tests.**

The order of these eight myths is deliberate. The first myth builds the foundation for the later myths by expanding the definition of what it means to know about assessment. Myths 2 through 5 discuss how the various kinds of assessment can be used effectively, such as classroom- and performance-based tests, multiple choice questions, and integrated skills assessments. The last three myths (6, 7, and 8) focus on theoretical and philosophical issues that have practical implications. They renew emphasis on the importance of topics in the earlier chapters. We hope that, by addressing eight beliefs about language assessment, this book will provide helpful insights into language assessment and instruction.

Key Terms in Language Testing

Throughout this book, several terms are important to general understanding of testing as well as to specific myths. This section explains a number of key ideas in broad terms because most of them will be developed and illustrated in later chapters. These terms are grouped in three categories: testing purposes, paired terms, and development and use of assessment in educational contexts.

TESTING PURPOSES

Each type of assessment fulfills different needs of teachers and language programs. It is critical to recognize the purpose of a test to appropriately develop or select a measure to fit one or more of these objectives:

- **Diagnostic:** This type of assessment is used to determine students' specific strengths and weaknesses during an instructional program. It helps teachers plan a path of improvement for each learner. These tests need to be aligned with the course curriculum and goals. Teachers can use the test results of the whole class to make decisions as to which aspects of language they will focus on and what are less important concerns for their students.
- **Placement:** A placement exam helps identify a student's level of language competency to determine which

course or level is appropriate. Placement testing is common in language programs that offer different levels of a language course. It is challenging because test-takers will have a range of abilities in the target language, such as having good reading skills but weak speaking proficiency. Combining students with different proficiency profiles into a course level so that all of them are well served is a tricky business. Teachers are often involved in placement testing, serving as proctors, raters, or even decision-makers.

- **Achievement:** These tests are developed to assess students' learning of coursework or other curriculum materials. They are closely aligned to course or program objectives and are often used at the end of a learning sequence. Achievement tests are among the most relevant for classroom teachers.

- **Proficiency:** Such general tests of language ability are often developed for large-scale testing without planned alignment to specific learning goals or language programs. Specific proficiency examinations, such as TOEFL® and IELTS®, serve as an admission requirement for non-native English speakers at many colleges and universities that use English as the medium for instruction. Government agencies, licensing bodies, businesses, and other institutions may also mandate proficiency tests. Teachers usually encounter proficiency tests when the administration of their institution requires a specific score from applicants for entry.

PAIRED TERMS

Quite a few terms in the field of assessment are paired because they are related and, in many cases, because they are contrasting concepts. Learning these terms together can be useful for comprehension and can illuminate important controversies in language testing.

- **Formative assessment** versus **summative assessment:** Formative assessment is used routinely in classrooms to reveal whether the students are mastering the learning objectives (see Myth 2). It generates information to gauge progress and helps improve learning and teaching throughout the course. Summative assessment provides information on learners' achievement at the end of a course or program.

- **High-stakes/standardized testing** versus **classroom-based assessment:** Any test that is given in the same manner to all test-takers can be considered a standardized test. We tend to contrast assessment used for high-stakes decisions developed by large publishers or testing organizations with assessment that is used or developed by individual teachers for classroom purposes with their particular students.

- **Selected response** versus **constructed response:** This distinction is about different kinds of test tasks. Selected-response test items require students to choose the correct answer, for example, in multiple choice questions or matching tasks. Constructed-response tasks ask test-takers to create or develop a response, either in a sentence or in longer spoken or written responses. Selected-response items are frequently used in large-scale testing for efficiency; however, in classroom assessments, constructed-response tasks are likely to be more meaningful, depending on course goals.

- **Performance assessment** versus **objective assessment:** Performance assessments include essay-writing or oral interviews, while objective assessments are generally selected-response items. The primary difference is in scoring: although some responses can be scored objectively when there is a right or wrong answer, performance assessment requires rating, which makes subjectivity possible and therefore complicates scoring.

If teachers use a performance assessment, such as an interview or essay, they need to be careful about consistency and fairness in how they score students' work.

- **Independent** versus **integrated skills assessment:** This pairing is about the kind of language being assessed. When reading, writing, listening, or speaking as an individual skill is the main focus of a test and the score will reflect ability in that particular skill, then it is **independent skills** assessment. On the other hand, if skills are combined, such as reading with writing or listening with speaking, then it is called **integrated skills** assessment. Choosing between these two approaches depends on the purpose of the assessment and the kind of language students will need to use in the future. If they need to combine skills, then integrated assessment is a good choice.

- **Validity** and **reliability:** Validity has to do with the confidence we have in our interpretations of test scores, while reliability is the consistency of those scores. Validity is important in deciding what meaning can be placed on the test results. For example, a test of speaking proficiency that requires test-takers to read and circle answers to multiple choice questions wouldn't have much validity. Reliability concerns the degree to which a test produces stable, consistent results. Factors affecting the reliability of a test include its length, whether it's scored objectively or subjectively, who the students are who are taking it, and what types of questions are included. Both of these concepts are important to ensure our assessments are of good quality and allow us to interpret the scores meaningfully. They are related to issues of fairness and accuracy, which are as important in classroom assessments as they are in standardized tests.

Development and Use of Assessment in Educational Contexts

The last group of terms are those commonly used in educational contexts to talk about the development and use of assessments.

- **Rubrics/rating scales:** Scoring scales are used to evaluate performances. They include criteria for a performance, descriptors of those criteria, and a scheme to arrive at a score. They can be used to improve the efficiency, fairness, and clarity of scores as well as to provide useful feedback on students' strengths and weaknesses.

- **Item analysis:** These procedures are for checking that test questions are at the right level of difficulty and that they distinguish test-takers appropriately. For example, if students who have a low overall score on a test get a certain item correct more often than higher-scoring students, this item needs to be rewritten. If a certain item is answered incorrectly by all test-takers, it might also be one that should be removed or rewritten. Item analysis also includes checking for biased questions and other problems that can occur in item writing. This process is done systematically on large-scale tests that use selected-response items and involves statistical analysis.

- **Score interpretation:** It is rare in language testing to assess language with the precision of measurement devices such as thermometers and rulers. Nevertheless, language assessment usually results in a number (score) that is used to reflect or interpret something about a student's language ability. While numbers are needed to provide students, teachers, and other stakeholders with a scale on which to evaluate improvement or general proficiency, it is important to remember that the number (score) itself does **not** carry meaning about a student's ability. Instead, the way we interpret that score is what gives it meaning. For example, 80 out of 100 only gives us a ratio or percentage, but in the context of a test, it could mean a student should be placed in a high-intermediate class, or it could mean that the student's English is good enough for academic coursework. It could also mean that the student has been successful in meeting course goals or that a pre-service teacher needs to improve his or her language skills before qualifying to teach English.

- **Construct:** A construct is a theoretical model of the underlying ability we are trying to assess. Constructs can be based on research or they may be based on a curriculum or syllabus. For example, the construct for second language reading might be defined with two major components: fluency and comprehension, which may be further subdivided into the skills and strategies of vocabulary recognition, inference-making, prediction, or first-language transfer. Defining the construct should be the first step in developing an assessment, and it must be aligned with the test's purpose.

- **Test washback:** Washback is the impact of a particular test on teachers, students, classrooms, and the outside world. Washback can be positive or negative. Negative washback occurs when a test undermines teaching and detracts from quality learning. Conversely, positive washback comes about when a test is well aligned with a course, thus supporting and motivating teachers and students.

- **Bias:** In assessments, when an individual or group of test-takers has certain characteristics that are not part of the construct being assessed and that give an unfair advantage, we say the test is biased in their favor. Or, the test may be biased to the detriment of some students. An example of bias might be when language assessment shows performance patterns that follow gender lines (female students scoring higher than male students or vice versa). In such cases, the assessment needs careful scrutiny to ensure that test items or tasks are not biased and did not cause such a pattern.

Throughout this book's exploration of myths in language testing, we hope readers will gain insight in the field as well as useful ideas for their teaching. Assessment holds a permanent position in teaching and learning, and the more teachers can leverage it to support their students and their classroom practice, the better. We wrote the chapters of this book with this purpose in mind.

Assessment is just writing tests and using statistics.

During my first years of teaching, I had a strong aversion to the word *test*. (This story is from Lia.) It got to the point that I was avoiding a required language testing course in my MA TESOL program. Mathematics had been difficult for me in high school and college, which made me worry about the statistics involved in this course. I was sure my grades would plummet. In addition, I was exasperated by pressure from students in my courses in the intensive English program (IEP). They regularly requested that I "teach them TOEFL®" (Test of English as a Foreign Language) rather than complete my carefully designed communicative language tasks. Finally, the last semester before graduating, I registered for the assessment course. It turned out to be a real eye-opener. While we did spend one day in a computer lab using a software program and some test data to run item analysis on multiple choice questions, most of the course focused on issues that were very meaningful to my classroom teaching: how to introduce students to peer and self-assessment, how to use rubrics to evaluate speaking and writing, and how to use constructs to underlie assessments.

This course helped me recognize that my definition of language assessment (and what I should learn about it) had been too narrow and was colored by my prior aversion to math and experiences with negative washback from a high-stakes test.

What the Research Says . . .

Undeniably, writing tests and analyzing their results is part of being a teacher, but many other things are equally important, if not more so, in understanding language assessment. Every day in language classrooms, assessment happens that is not what most people would consider testing. Assessment can be a less formal gathering of information, such as checking in with students and altering lessons based on their progress. Assessment may be teachers using small group discussions about a course reading to listen for development of oral skills. Assessment can be students answering scaffolding questions as they complete a task to see how they learn with some mediated support. Short quickwrites can be assessments—informing teachers what a student has learned from a lesson and what else he or she want to know.

Teachers are also involved in assessment whenever they make decisions about which tests to use; how to interpret scores; or the best ways to communicate results to students, parents, administrators, and other stakeholders. All these daily activities go beyond writing items and scoring. Inbar-Lourie (2008) describes the teachers' process: "Being literate in assessment thus means having the capacity to ask and answer critical questions about the purpose for assessment, about the fitness of the tool being used, about testing conditions, and about what is going to happen on the basis of the results" (p. 389).

What Should Teachers Know?

Several scholars and professional organizations have attempted to clarify what teachers need to know about assessment. This goal is complicated because a perceived, and at times, real divide exists between large-scale standardized tests and more context-driven local assessments used by teachers (Inbar-Lourie, 2008; Malone, 2013; McNamara & Roever, 2006; Scarino, 2013; Shepard, 2000). Assessment in learning contexts considers both learning outcomes and processes and is seen as inseparable from instruction. However, teachers also need to be able to interpret and use more formal tests for diagnostic, placement, and exit decisions. These varied demands require some understanding of classroom-based assessment and large-scale standardized tests (Inbar-Lourie, 2008). Teachers need to balance external information and internal input, an ability that requires assessment literacy (Taylor, 2010).

Besides the fundamentals of test development, equally important are issues related to the *use* of assessment, such as how to interpret scores, consider validity and reliability, advocate for ethical decision-making, and understand consequences. This dynamic is explained as understanding the *what* and *how,* as well as the *why,* of language assessment (Inbar-Lourie, 2008). The use-related aspects reflect social contexts of assessment, which can be more opaque than the procedures of test development.

A number of U.S. organizations have collaborated in developing seven standards for teacher competence in assessment in general, not just specific to language learning. This list shown in Figure 1.1 offers valuable insights into what constitutes assessment literacy for teachers.

While the second and third standards address test development, the other five deal with practical issues involved in using tests, such as choosing and making decisions about tests and the social aspects of communicating results and considering ethical uses.

FIGURE 1.1: Standards for Teacher Competence in Educational Assessment of Students

Teachers should be skilled in:

1. choosing assessment methods appropriate for instructional decisions
2. developing assessment methods appropriate for instructional decisions
3. administering, scoring, and interpreting the results of both externally produced and teacher-produced assessment methods
4. using assessment results when making decisions about individual students, planning teaching, developing curriculum, and improving schools
5. developing valid pupil grading procedures, which use assessment
6. communicating assessment results to students, parents, other lay audiences, and other educators
7. recognizing unethical, illegal, and otherwise inappropriate assessment methods and uses of assessment information.

Source: American Federation of Teachers, National Council on Measurement in Education, and National Education Association, 1990, pages 4–6.

These standards present general guidelines for teachers' competence in assessment; however, we need to consider the *language* issue in language assessment literacy (Inbar-Lourie, 2013; Taylor, 2010, 2013). Language assessment also includes understanding how evaluation impacts learning and contexts. Teachers need a solid understanding of the theories that shape the content of language assessment (Inbar-Lourie, 2008). For example, we emphasize **communicative competence** or **intercultural competence** in language teaching, but what exactly are the components of these constructs, and how are they elicited by our classroom assessments? Language assessment literacy includes knowing the theory well enough to use it for test development and score interpretation. Teachers also need a solid grounding in methodology that will allow them to connect assessment and up-to-date approaches to language learning. For example, teachers adhering to the principles of Communicative Language Teaching (CLT) will select and develop tests that support this method and will bypass the sort of multiple choice grammar tests that contribute little to the CLT curriculum.

How Is Language Assessment Taught?

While standards and competencies attempt to identify what teachers should know, research has looked at how language assessment is taught by analyzing surveys and interviews with faculty who are teaching the testing courses. Brown and Bailey conducted studies in 1996 and 2008 to explore the content of language testing courses in ESL/EFL teacher training. In their 2008 web-based study, they surveyed 97 instructors of language testing courses in 11 countries. The survey consisted of 96 Likert-scale questions regarding the instructors, the course content, and students' attitudes. Results of the survey revealed a number of topics commonly covered in language testing courses. The ten general topics listed scored above an average mean (M) of 2.55 on a five-point Likert scale:

- Testing within the language course curriculum ($M=3.26$)
- Classroom testing practice ($M=3.23$)
- How to measure different skills ($M=3.19$)
- Criterion-referenced testing ($M=2.99$)
- Achievement testing* ($M=2.92$)
- Washback*/test impact ($M=2.86$)
- Proficiency testing* ($M=2.83$)
- Alternative assessment procedures ($M=2.74$)
- How to assess at different language proficiency levels ($M=2.63$)
- Critiquing published tests ($M=2.56$)

(Topics with an asterisk * were defined in our Introduction; others appear in a box in this chapter.)

All ten topics are clearly relevant to language teachers: several relate to the purpose of testing (achievement, proficiency) while others center on test content (skills, criterion-reference, levels, alternative assessments). Two that are highly relevant to test use and fairness are washback and testing within the curriculum. These results indicate that language testing courses are addressing many of the areas defined as important for teachers' assessment literacy and according to standards for teacher development.

More Important Assessment Definitions

Criterion-referenced assessment: This relates to instructional decisions. Have the test-takers learned or achieved a certain standard? For example, course objectives may be criteria measured by an end-of-course exam.

Norm-referenced assessment: This type of test compares groups of individuals. For example, the GRE® test is norm-referenced because an individual's score is reported in relation to those of the other test-takers. This approach is common for high-stakes testing that seeks to differentiate test-takers for decision-making purposes, such as deciding which students to admit to universities.

Alternative assessment: This applies to testing that differs from the traditional forms, portfolios or self-assessments.

Test specifications: The blueprint for a particular test starts with a general description and articulates its objectives and the attributes of prompts and responses (such as length, medium, delivery), as well as sample items, scoring procedures, and ways to interpret scores.

Accommodations: These supports try to minimize factors that affect test responses outside the desired trait being measured. For example, if an English language learner is taking a mathematics exam in English, accommodations might be provided to ensure that only math is being tested, not the student's English ability. For example, the test directions may be given in a student's native language, a bilingual dictionary may be allowed, or extra time may be given to complete the test.

A study by Jeong (2013) compared language testing course instructors who were language testing professionals with instructors who were not. The study used mixed research methods: a survey of 140 instructors and in-depth interviews with 13 of them. Jeong found that the structure and organization of language testing courses were the same for both groups. The five topics that instructors spent the most time on were test theory, classroom assessment, alternative performance assessments, test specifications, and rubric development. However, the two groups differed on the issue of accommodations, with the instructors who were not language testing professionals seeing this topic as more important. Jeong's interviews revealed that several non-language testing professionals believed that current textbooks in language testing focused too much on large-scale testing and were too difficult for pre-service student teachers in their courses. Apparent from this study is that the background of the instructor may impact the areas emphasized in a language assessment course but, in general, language testing courses for teachers need to focus on issues relevant to classroom assessment and not just statistics or test writing.

Language teachers' perspectives of assessment literacy coursework differ from that of standards and instructors and perhaps illuminate the origin of this myth. Fulcher (2012) surveyed 278 university-level language teachers to uncover what assessment training they believed they needed to be successful. Eighty percent of the respondents said they had studied topics related to large-scale assessment in language testing courses, and nearly all listed "test analysis" as part of their studies. Interestingly, in response to a question about what they needed to know more about, statistics was most frequently cited; 35 percent said they wanted to understand statistics "conceptually." There was also strong interest in how to check for reliability and validity in the test development process; 26 percent of the respondents wanted to learn more about the stages of test development. This study found that teachers believed that the principles of language testing are as important as more practical knowledge and that training should include both. Based on his results, Fulcher (2012) defined language assessment literacy as:

> the knowledge, skills and abilities required to design, develop, maintain or evaluate large-scale standardized and/or classroom-based tests, familiarity with test processes, and awareness of principles and concepts that guide and underpin practice, including ethics and codes of practice. [It is also] the ability to place knowledge, skills, processes, principles and concepts within wider historical, social, political and philosophical frameworks in order to understand why practices have arisen as they have, and to evaluate the role and impact of testing on society, institutions, and individuals. (p. 125)

What We Can Do . . .

Various avenues exist for developing assessment literacy through practice, but they require time and attention, which can be a challenge considering all the other demands on teachers. Davison (2004) describes the dilemma this way:

> Teachers need explicit high-quality assessment criteria as a framework for dialogue. They also need time and space to develop a sense of ownership and common understanding of the assessment process and to articulate and critique their often implicit constructs and interpretations. Such teacher interactions are also necessary to help all stake-holders develop a more informed perspective of teacher assessment practices and to establish the key ingredients for validity and reliability in teacher-based assessment: dialogue and trust. (p. 328)

1. Think inclusively about assessment.

The first step in expanding our understanding of assessment is to consider it as more than just tests and quizzes. Many activities in our classes serve the purpose of evaluating students' understanding, such as judging whether certain course objectives have been met, informing students about the learning that is happening in the classroom, and marking their homework. All these activities are forms of assessment, and we need to consider carefully and systematically how we use them to make decisions. Offering feedback and scoring student work should be grounded in what we know about teaching and learning. If we recognize the pervasive role of assessment in our classrooms, then we will develop the habit of seriously integrating it into our planning and daily routines. All of these aspects of assessment should be included in teacher development.

2. Collaborate on assessment development and dilemmas.

Collaborating when developing language tests also increases assessment knowledge and experience. Teachers can form working groups to develop tests together or work on problems created by assessments in their contexts. Deliberating on the challenges and decisions required to create, implement, and use a test with a fellow teacher can encourage innovative ways of thinking about assessment. For example, instructors teaching multiple sections of the same course can meet throughout the term to discuss what kinds of assessments they are using and to collaborate on developing a rubric to use across sections. Working together makes assessments stronger and has the added benefit of bringing teachers together to talk about the basic goals of learning and teaching.

3. Build assessment literacy through learning communities and collaboration.

Since teachers are lifelong learners and assessment literacy is part of their developing knowledge, finding venues for continued professional development is imperative. One route is to employ Professional Learning Communities (PLCs), which are semi-formal working groups of colleagues. PLCs can be top-down (set up by administrators) or bottom-up (individuals come together to work on a common goal). They can also be formed online, allowing PLCs to develop beyond a local context, so teachers and scholars can interact more broadly and across contexts. Another approach to shared professional development is an inquiry group. It may narrow its focus to research and scholarship in a particular area and meet regularly to explore topics together. Starting a PLC or an inquiry group around issues of assessment literacy provides opportunities to build knowledge collaboratively by sharing insights, experiences, and resources. To seek more information on topics brought up in inquiry groups, teachers can consult the major assessment journals (*Language Assessment Quarterly*, *Language Testing*, or *Assessing Writing*), as well as richly developed websites such as Language Testing Resources (http://languagetesting.info/).

MYTH **2**

A comprehensive final exam is the best way to evaluate students.

In college, I took German for three years, earning very average grades. (This is Lia.) As a reward for my persistence, I studied in Austria for a semester to experience German-speaking culture and "authentic" language. During that semester, I was greatly surprised to learn that my German was more than adequate for basic communication and that I could spend hours in conversation using only German with my host mother. By the last month of my stay, shopkeepers no longer answered my questions in English and they conversed with me in German. As I was departing Austria, I was able to arrange, in German, for my suitcase to precede me on a train to Belgium. I was delighted to find it waiting at the station when I arrived.

I had more success using my German when traveling abroad than I'd expected based on my grades in college classes. This seemed like a mismatch because I felt my classes prepared me well in authentic German; I'd spent four days a week in class talking about topics such as family, school, and travel. Although the first two years of coursework followed a communicative syllabus, 75 percent of my grade was based on an end-of-semester final. This exam was strictly grammar-based, administered to all sections of German at the same time, and graded uniformly. It was given in a large, crowded auditorium. I was elbow-to-elbow with other students, and all of us were filling in bubble sheets. The conclusion that I came to about my language skills was that my German was okay, but my grades reflected that I was bad at tests. In-class assessments were occasional quizzes modeled on the final exam. This disconnect was a problem for us as students in understanding the goals of the course and in interpreting our grades. Without regular assessment parallel to class activities, we lost the opportunity to gauge and guide our language learning. If I had not studied abroad, I would have simply assumed that I had never really learned German.

What the Research Says . . .

Since the 1960s, a distinction has been made between two kinds of assessment: formative and summative (Shavelson et al., 2008). **Summative assessments** evaluate cumulative knowledge or abilities usually at the end of a learning sequence, such as final comprehensive exams. **Formative assessments** are frequent checkpoints embedded in the context of the course that evaluate learning both formally and informally. Their purpose is to help learners and teachers check progress and also to steer them toward meeting course goals. Formative and summative assessments are not unrelated and exist on a continuum rather than being strictly dichotomous (Black, Harrison, Lee, Marshall, & Williams, 2003; Shavelson et al., 2008; Stiggins, 2005)—for example, a midterm exam could be used for both formative and summative purposes.

Ideally, the two kinds of assessments share an underlying model of language and learning, called a **construct** (see page 10 for a definition). Both should be related to course goals and objectives as well as the same vision of language learning. In fact, summative and formative assessments that inform each other are the most effective and expedient. Figure 2.1 lists examples of each type of assessment. While the ten-

FIGURE 2.1: Examples of Formative and Summative Assessment in Language Learning

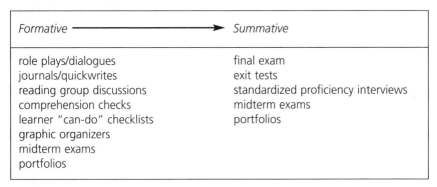

Formative ⟶	Summative
role plays/dialogues journals/quickwrites reading group discussions comprehension checks learner "can-do" checklists graphic organizers midterm exams portfolios	final exam exit tests standardized proficiency interviews midterm exams portfolios

dency is to judge one as more valuable than the other, the best practice is for both to have a place in education and to be aligned.

Formative Assessment

Formative assessment has several unique characteristics. First, it is a frequent, ongoing part of instruction, even when it takes an abbreviated form. Second, it informs both teachers and students of progress being made. This progress can be captured for individual learners as well as subgroups and whole classes. Formative assessment identifies gaps between what students know and can do and what they need to know and be able to do. Finding and filling this gap is an important step in learner-centered instruction. The goal for formative assessment is to improve learning, rather than to judge individual achievement. If students understand this characteristic of formative assessment, they may be less anxious and perform closer to their actual ability. Last, due to the possibility of individualizing formative assessment and its outcomes, this kind of assessment is adaptive and allows for differentiation, something particularly critical in classrooms where students often have a wide range of language abilities.

Shavelson et al. (2008) provide a scale for types of formative assessment. On one end are "on-the-fly" assessments, which include such teachable moments as when a teacher overhears or notices student interactions that reveal a gap in learning. At the other end of the scale is **embedded assessment,** or structured inventories aligning specific learning goals with curricular objectives. Between these two extremes are planned-for interaction and exchanges targeting certain learning objectives, such as a series of questions posed during class discussions. Considering assessment at all these levels opens up possibilities for continually collecting information about students' learning and for addressing gaps before the end of the term/program when it is too late to remedy them.

Black et al. (2003) reviewed four recent developments in formative assessment practices that can be useful for teachers to consider. The first is attending to classroom dialogue as a means to guide assessment and give feedback. In this case, the teacher listens in on group work to observe the students' language use and to notice where and why communication breakdowns occur. Another area of increasing attention in formative assessment is peer and self-assessment, which engage students in the evaluation of their learning. A third area, specifically in writing, is the use of "comment-only" marking or writing conferences (one-on-one discussions of writing), which emphasize feedback in the absence of a grade. It removes judgment and focuses on the students' improvement. The fourth development described by Black et al. (2003) is the use of summative tests in formative ways. This approach entails including some aspects of final or standardized tests in classroom assessment but with lower stakes and a different emphasis. Teachers can provide learners with test items or tasks and then use them to discuss model performances or engage in other guided activities.

Classroom-Based Assessment for Language Teaching

Scholars have discussed the difference between assessment **of** learning and assessment **for** learning (Colby-Kelly & Turner, 2007; Leung, 2007). Substituting the preposition **for** distinguishes assessment embedded in the learning processes from assessment focused outside of it. A final exam that evaluates the knowledge students have absorbed by the end of the coursework would be an assessment **of** learning.

Contrast that with this example of assessment *for* learning: Students are assigned to write the questions for a chapter test that requires them to think about what they should have learned from the material. Then they critique the questions in class and develop an answer key. These activities would focus students on learning goals and their progress toward them. A third variant on this theme is assessment *as* learning (Earl & Katz, 2006), which sees assessment as encouraging students' metacognitive thinking about their learning. It creates an atmosphere where students are active in thinking about and evaluating their learning to make decisions based on their progress.

A similar pairing is between **dynamic** assessment and **static** assessment. Again, a final exam would exemplify **static** assessment; once teachers have developed or adopted a final exam, the test will remain the same when all students take it. A **dynamic** assessment could be a test, too, but one that includes interaction between the teacher and students. During such assessment, the teacher provides guidance to help a student proceed. It is not just about correct or incorrect answers but about how a student engages when support, or scaffolding, comes from the teacher, who models the process of learning.

From these two dichotomies come two approaches related to assessment in language learning classrooms: **Assessment for Learning** (AfL) and **Dynamic Assessment** (DA). Neither approach is unique to language teaching; each has a history in the field of education. Yet over the past decade, national ministries of education, school districts, curriculum developers, and researchers have increased the amount of attention both of these approaches have received.

ASSESSMENT FOR LEARNING (AfL)

The Assessment Reform Group (2002) in the U.K. emphasized the goal of AfL as "the process of seeking and interpreting evidence for use by learners and their teachers to decide where learners are in their learning, where they need to go, and how best to get there." AfL views assessment as a tool rather than simply a measure of learning. It focuses on the relationship across teaching, learning, and assessment—

in particular, how assessment can be used to inform both teaching and learning (Lee, 2007b).

Process writing is an example of AfL that has been widely accepted in second language teaching. In this approach, students work through multiple drafts of their writing projects and receive feedback at each stage. Peer review is often incorporated to provide additional feedback. While serving as reviewers of each other's writing, students develop critical judgment and awareness of the criteria for good writing. An example of AfL from a second grade ESL classroom is the use of signal cards to check comprehension: Each child has three cards colored red, green, or yellow on his or her desk. Periodically during a lesson, the teacher asks the learners about their understanding of the lesson, and they each hold up a card showing that they do not understand (red), need more time (yellow), or are ready to move on (green). This showing of cards gives the teacher a quick and visible way to check in with learners; in addition, it does not require a great deal of language, which can facilitate communication for young learners and those at a beginning level of English proficiency.

A number of research studies have looked at AfL in second language classrooms (Colby-Kelly & Turner, 2007; Ellery, 2008; Lee, 2007a, 2007b). Based on this research, formative assessment and AfL appear to be recognized and valued by teachers in general. Yet when practice and perceptions are thoroughly investigated, classroom assessment still seems teacher-directed and overshadowed by summative feedback. Thus, the potential learning opportunity that AfL affords is shortchanged.

Colby-Kelly and Turner (2007) studied a pre-university English for Academic Purposes (EAP) program that had integrated AfL into its curriculum. Specifically, the study focused on the assessment of speaking performances and feedback. Researchers collected data from nine teachers and 42 students and found substantial use of AfL by teachers, particularly in feedback to students. Although teachers reported strong support for this type of assessment, the researchers found that feedback was most often between the teacher and an individual student, rather than between the teacher and groups or among peers. Such feedback was given privately and discreetly, as if it were something negative that might embarrass students. Teachers were also hesitant in their views regarding the usefulness of peer and self-assessment. Despite having a clear plan for AfL, the teachers' interpretation of feedback seemed at times to contrast with the spirit of AfL, which is to help learners see the benefits of others' input as a natural part of learning. The message from assessment needs to be on learning how to learn, not simply on being judged.

As previously mentioned, second language writing classrooms that have adopted a process approach to teaching writing are already using AfL (Ellery, 2008). In a research study, Lee (2007b) investigated the function of feedback in AfL. She collected feedback from 26 teachers on more than 174 writing assignments from secondary classrooms and then interviewed both students and teachers. She used six characteristics of AfL to analyze the teachers' feedback and found that their comments tended to focus more on summative assessment and error correction. Such negative feedback led to generalizations with little concrete meaning to students. In interviews with these teachers, they explained this tendency as a response to substantial pressure in a highly exam-focused educational system. This top-down pressure included emphasis on accuracy in written products, which was also conveyed by the teachers in their feedback. Student involvement in assessment was minimal; even more distressing, the teachers admitted that their feedback was probably not that useful to students. Lee (2007b) emphasizes the need to seek the overlap between exams and classroom assessment in AfL; in the contexts she studied, the two remained separate, and as a result, high-stakes exams seemed to drive the teaching and assessment in the classroom in an unproductive manner.

Assessment for Learning is a detailed plan to integrate formative assessment and involve learners in the learning process. It entails a commitment from teachers to guide students to become self-assessors, which requires practice, modeling, and time. Ideally, AfL is adopted from the beginning of a learning sequence or grade level, so that it is not just one class or one teacher trying to make this significant change in how assessment is perceived and what roles teacher and student perform in this endeavor.

DYNAMIC ASSESSMENT

Dynamic Assessment (DA) came to the field of education from the concept in sociocultural theory. The Zone of Proximal Development (ZPD), an idea attributed to Lev Vygotsky, maintains that a novice learner will progress better with the guidance of an expert than he or she will alone. Lantolf and Poehner have brought the idea of DA to the field of language learning through a number of theoretical and practice-focused articles (Lantolf & Poehner, 2007; Poehner, 2007, 2008, 2009; Poehner & Lantolf, 2005).

Dynamic assessment allows us to gauge a learner's ability to respond to assistance by a teacher or someone guiding the learner. Assessment and mediation are fully integrated, which gives the learner support to complete a learning unit. The teacher's intervention is part of the assessment, and DA is used to evaluate the student's response. This information allows us to measure how learners will learn, as well as how they can perform the task after receiving some guidance. Another critical aspect of DA is how well learners are able to transfer what they gained from the intervention to other situations. DA, then, is not a single-shot assessment but is continuous and iterative throughout the term.

In DA, the teacher guides the students with leading questions to help structure their thinking about a problem or task. Articles by Poehner provide many examples of DA in foreign language classrooms when it is expanded to groups and the whole class (Poehner, 2009; Poehner & Compernolle, 2011). DA can be illustrated by a teacher-to-student interaction. This example is from a writing conference, Lia observed. Notice how mediation is used to guide the language learner.

> S: [Reading essay aloud] The person I admire is no here. She is my mother.
> T: Is *no here* important to know? I mean, what is most important in this opening sentence? The person or the location?

S: No here. She's not here. She is in away.

T: What is most important to know first, *who* you admire or *where* that person is?

S: Who. My mother.

T: So could you put that in the first sentence?

S: The person I admire is my mother. She is no here.

T: What about *no here*? Is *no* the right form?

S: No, *not*. . . . She is not here.

T: Great! Let's move forward.

Oskoz (2005) investigated the use of DA to evaluate synchronous computer-mediated communication (SCMC) in foreign language classrooms, such as in online chatting. She explains that SCMC is a process-oriented learning activity, and so assessment used with such interaction should be focused on process, rather than just the product, making DA a natural fit. In her study of five university-level Spanish classes, students were recorded interacting through online activities, such as information gaps and jigsaw puzzles. These interactions were analyzed using a five-level scale adapted from previous research to evaluate learners' attention to and correction of errors. Using this scale, Oskoz considered how the SCMC transcripts indicate a learner's level in terms of self-error correction as well as responses to a partner's guidance in recognizing and selecting errors. In her conclusion, Oskoz establishes that DA has the potential to provide rich information for evaluating students' interlanguage development through SCMC. This finding suggests that DA is well suited to certain kinds of tasks or classroom activities, particularly those that emphasize process.

Kozulin and Garb (2004) conducted a DA study following a testing-learning-testing format in a language program in Israel with 13 English-as-a-third-language learners from Ethiopia. These students started with a pre-test session using six items from a standardized placement test. A mediation session followed in which the pre-test material was discussed in relation to the students' pre-existing knowledge and what strategies they would need to answer the test items. A post-test had similar items with different content from the pre-test. Not surprisingly, these learners did better on the post-test once the mediation had occurred but, more important, the researchers could observe which learners benefited most from the mediation. Analyzing the change in scores from pre- to post-test provided information on a student's learning potential and his or her individual learning needs. Although Kozulin and Garb (2004) admit that DA may be more time consuming to carry out than static testing, with mediation incorporated into classroom learning, this difference may disappear. They see DA as a critical process in understanding students' learning needs and highlight the need to prepare teachers as mediators. This aspect of DA is an important one to consider because the mediation depends on teachers providing useful input and feedback rather than teachers simply just correcting students or giving them answers.

Advocates of the DA approach believe that it allows for a more nuanced understanding of learners' development. It is less structured in terms of beginning and ending measures with more focus on the interactions that occur throughout the intervention. While we are including DA in a chapter with formative assessment, DA proponents claim that there is a distinction between these two approaches: DA should always be systematic, and although formative assessment is often planned, it can also be more spontaneous. DA is directed at long-term development, which highlights its similarities to AfL. DA and AfL embody different approaches to assessing students even though they both promote learning that shifts away from the traditional comprehensive final exam. They offer teachers insight into learners' progress and create new ways to evaluate and individualize instruction. AfL brings students into the assessment process to promote lifelong learning skills. DA brings assessment and teacher scaffolding into close proximity. In both approaches, assessment is ongoing and iterative throughout a term. Implementing DA or AfL should be done with curricular goals in mind and with deliberate consideration of alignment with summative assessment as well as other standardized testing used to evaluate learners.

What We Can Do . . .

Research shows that classroom-based assessment provides valuable information about learning and development to both teachers and learners, making it an insightful part of language teaching. How can we make it part of daily classroom activities?

1. Create an ongoing cycle of assessment, instruction, and course goals.

Planning should promote continuity between summative and formative assessment and also provide useful checkpoints on students' progress throughout the term. It is better to know by Week 5 that students are not able to write complex sentences or that they have not grasped the past perfect tense than to make such a discovery at the end of the term when there is no time to remedy it. Best practices in formative assessment require planning at the outset and continuous monitoring as the course progresses. Figure 2.2 illustrates this process. Notice the double arrows on the right side of the figure, moving back and forth between weekly course objectives, instructional planning, and formative assessment. These three activities support and inform each other. With summative assessment, the process tends to be more linear.

FIGURE 2.2: Assessment in Curriculum Planning

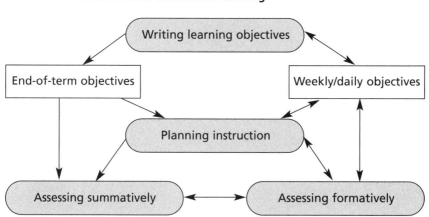

As part of developing their classes, teachers should incorporate an assessment plan. This plan should mesh with the daily lesson plans of a course, which are aligned with the overall curriculum of the course. An assessment plan could take many forms, but it must be a useful reference for the instructor. Aspects to include in the plan are: instructional objectives, assessments and activities, and procedures for scoring and providing feedback (see an example in Table 2.1).

The plan in Table 2.1 illustrates the alignment between assessment and instruction. In the example, the teacher has distinguished between activities, assessments, and feedback/scoring; marked those assessments that will be scored for grading; and included three uses for the results. The level of detail and categories depends on the teacher's needs and style. However, the plan should be followed closely through-

TABLE 2.1: An Assessment Plan for a Second Language Writing Class

Instructional Objective	Activities (A)	Assessments (Aa)	Scoring & Feedback	Decisions
Developing summarization skills	A1. Whole class model of summary writing A2. Pairs practice summary writing A3. Whole class critiques pairs' summaries	Aa1. Student highlights key ideas in reading Aa2. Student writes a summary in a template Aa3. Student writes an independent summary	Whole class builds rubric from critique of summary A3 Students use rubric to self-assess Aa2 & Aa3 Teacher uses rubric to score Aa3	A2 & A3 used to decide if students are ready for assessment Aa3 Results of self-assessment and Aa3 used to determine if more summary work is needed Score from Aa3 used for students' final grade

out the term, remembering that it is dynamic—changes can and should be made—but that such changes should be recorded in the plan.

In addition, such a plan can help teachers think through the instructional decisions that can be based on the assessments and eventually plan how to use the outcomes. Assessment can inform us of the progress of individual students and the class as a whole, as well as help us to decide how we teach a certain lesson in the future. Including these decisions in the assessment plan will help teachers remember all the information they have gleaned.

2. Emphasize the feedback aspect of assessment.

The research discussed shows the value of feedback in formative assessment, AfL, and DA. While a grade or a number communicates some information to learners and teachers, learning occurs when clear explanations and suggestions for improvement are provided. Giving useful feedback is a skill that teachers should cultivate and monitor. Finding ways to make comments comprehensible entails knowing what wording will be understood by language learners (especially second language learners). Having the class discuss grading criteria or rubrics is a way to increase the value of feedback later on. Giving examples of "good" performances can also guide learners. Activities that allow students practice using the assignment criteria can make expectations clearer. Some other approaches to emphasizing feedback include:

- Having one-on-one conferences with students to discuss their assessment performances. If students can lead the conversation in conferences, teachers might discover issues they hadn't considered, such as misunderstood expectations or confusion over language forms or functions.
- Requiring revisions based on feedback. Selective revisions require students to focus on one area for improvement, such as word variety when writing or fluency in speaking. Giving students an opportunity to

use the teacher's feedback for improvement comes through second chances. It also allows teachers to see how well students can use the feedback (mediation) to learn.

- Checking with students to learn whether the feedback being given is clear. Using jargon or abstract terminology can make feedback confusing and potentially useless. Examples of vague terms include: *awkward wording, conciseness,* or *misplaced modifier.* Give students an example and make sure the language used in feedback has been covered in class.

- Giving a new grade or revised grade based on improvements from feedback. While a long-term goal is to take emphasis off grades, students still care and see grades as indicators of what a teacher values. Rewarding attention to feedback with grading can increase, in students' eyes, the value of the feedback and the learning that is gained from following it.

Since these feedback practices may be more difficult to employ when class sizes are large, teachers must look for efficient strategies. Using a rubric that students are familiar with is one approach (this will be discussed in detail in Myth 3). Another is to incorporate peer and self-assessment after students have been trained to give helpful feedback. Although a good deal of work is required to establish this approach at the beginning of a course, it will pay off later on as students can become sources of feedback.

3. Involve students in the assessment process.

Students need time to learn which criteria are used in assessment and how to assess their own or others' work. Sharing models or examples is an effective method to train students on peer and self-assessment. It is also critical, especially initially, to help students see the value in this practice because some students may believe that the only important feedback comes from the teacher. One strategy from a writing classroom is to ask students to provide feedback to each other on early drafts. Then, as they rewrite, ask them to reflect on what input they used from peers in their own writing and how it changed their final paper.

In addition to peer and self-assessment, students can be asked to reflect on their learning throughout the course. While they may not be accustomed to thinking about it or articulating it, this can be cultivated through regular practice. Self-assessment can be as simple as the example of students holding up a red, yellow, or green card, indicating whether they are ready to move to a new topic. Another example could be asking students, as they prepare to hand in a major assignment, to write answers to three questions: What did you learn from this assignment? What would you like to practice more in the next assignment? What do you hope to learn as you complete the next assignment? This reflection can be a 15-minute quickwrite or even just some words or phrases to answer each question; whatever the method, it may provide useful information to the teacher.

Another way to involve students is to include them in the development of assessments and rubrics. Working in groups, students can create possible questions for a midterm and, later, the whole class can critique them. In designing and critiquing questions, students need to review important material from the course, consider how to elicit knowledge and abilities related to this content, and deliberate on what "correct" answers might be. This process provides many learning opportunities and results in a collaborative exam.

Another approach is to ask students to design a rubric for a performance assessment (see Myth 3 for more on performance assessment). Given examples of strong and weak performances, students in small groups discuss and place these performances in various categories. This technique could result in concrete criteria for evaluation. The teacher can monitor and mediate the process of collecting student-generated criteria. Issues can be highlighted, such as weighting criteria in a rubric (what is most important?) and discussing criteria that are difficult to measure. The activity culminates in the use of the rubric to evaluate students' assessment performances.

In all of these examples, it is important to realize that the first time students participate in assessment development, they may find it quite challenging and the results will not be perfect. Even for professional language testers, revision and reflection are critical parts of the assessment process. After a class-generated test is taken or a rubric used, students should review its success and learn from aspects that did not work as expected. Then the activities can be repeated, giving students an understanding of the evolution of their learning.

Scores on performance assessments are preferable because of their accuracy and authenticity.

In the Real World . . .

I had just started a new job in an IEP, and we were in the throes of placement testing. (This is another experience from Lia.) I was being trained to rate the program's writing test. For 30 minutes the students wrote an essay response to a prompt, and then for two to three hours the teachers had to read and rate the papers (usually 60–75 of them). The rating rubric used was a popular commercially available ESL composition scale totaling 100 points, which included points in five categories: organization, development, grammar, vocabulary, and mechanics. In explaining this rubric to me, the experienced instructors pointed out that the writing of students was much lower than the high end of the scale and that, if the scale were applied correctly, students in the program would have generally scored below the midpoint (50 of 100 points). They explained that, over the years, the scores had been pushed up to ensure there was a useful spread for placement. It was rather like starting a race three feet ahead of the starting line.

The process was mysterious to me at first but, after about an hour, I became accustomed to the practice. Although we raters might have more or less agreed with each other on the scores assigned, this procedure was clearly problematic. All of us were inflating the scores, but there was no assurance that we were doing so in the same way. We were re-interpreting the descriptors on the rubric individually as we rated. Therefore, the scoring no longer worked as it was meant to. How could we claim that our students' scores accurately assessed their true performance and placed them at the right level? Finding the right rating scale is one of the challenges commonly encountered by teachers when using performance assessment.

What the Research Says . . .

The enthusiasm for performance assessment in modern language testing may be attributed to at least two events: (1) a shift in the definition of language ability and (2) increased emphasis in the U.S. on assessing foreign language use by the government and large public institutions. Since the 1970s and '80s, language teaching and learning have gravitated toward the performance-centered idea of language ability called **communicative competence**. The term, originally used by anthropologist Dell Hymes (1972), was introduced to the field by Canale and Swain in 1980. Hymes defined communicative competence as what we say to whom, when, where, and in what manner. Canale and Swain further defined it as a composite of competences: grammatical, discourse, sociolinguistic, and strategic (see Figure 3.1). Assessing communicative competence is best done through performance and has led to a focus on direct approaches in testing speaking and writing as opposed to indirect methods using multiple choice or fill-in-the-blank test items.

FIGURE 3.1: Communicative Competence

Grammatical competence includes the linguistic rules of a language, particularly those of morphology, phonology, and syntax.

Discourse competence is the ability to connect ideas and sentences into meaningful discourse.

Sociolinguistic competence shows our understanding of the sociocultural rules of a language, such as what expressions are appropriate or not in a given situation with certain speakers.

Strategic competence covers communication and compensation strategies used in successful interactions. It includes what we say to repair communication breakdowns, such as guessing or paraphrasing when something is not understood.

Sources: Canale and Swain, 1980; Canale, 1983.

Another motivator of performance assessment in language testing in the United States came from its government, which needed to assess language in use (Chalhoub-Deville & Fulcher, 2003). The approach for measuring this was an oral interview, which required a scale to score the test-takers' spoken language (see Figure 3.2 on the difference between a rating scale and a rubric). The U.S. Department of State's Foreign Service Institute created an interview and scale for testing the language of personnel such as diplomats employed in embassies around the world. This scale became popular throughout government circles. However, challenges arose when it was adopted for use in different contexts and led representatives from various federal agencies to join forces to streamline the scale and develop new guidelines. The resulting Interagency Language Roundtable (ILR) scale uses descriptors to capture characteristics of oral language at different foreign language proficiency levels. Soon language programs in universities and public schools became interested in using the ILR scale, but the nature of this scale made it extremely difficult to adapt for non–intensive language programs. The ILR scale served best in contexts where students study language for almost 48 hours per week for periods ranging from one to four years. In contrast, in civilian educational settings, language is generally taught for only three to four hours per week.

FIGURE 3.2: The Difference Between Rating Scales and Rubrics

These two terms are sometimes used interchangeably and are certainly closely related. The distinction comes in the level of detail and, sometimes, in their purpose. A **rating scale** has the main goal of determining a score on a performance, while a **rubric** is often used in educational settings to provide feedback to students. Because of this difference, a scale may have less detail in the criteria for scoring and be more concise in describing different levels of performance. Since rubrics are often given to students to understand their strengths and weaknesses to improve, the criteria and descriptors need to be more transparent and concrete.

As a result, a new set of performance scales were developed by the American Council on the Teaching of Foreign Languages (ACTFL) to address the needs of non–intensive foreign language programs in educational settings. The ACTFL Guidelines include four main levels: novice, intermediate, advanced, and superior (recently a fifth level was added—distinguished). The first three levels are divided into three sublevels: low, mid, and high, which results in ten ACTFL levels. ACTFL Guidelines were also written for skills such as reading and writing, even though the initial goal was for rating oral performances from the Oral Proficiency Interview (OPI). These guidelines, which have been revised several times, are available online at the ACTFL website (http://actflproficiencyguidelines2012.org/). Used mostly for performance assessment, these guidelines have positioned this mode of assessing language, particularly oral interviews, at the forefront of foreign language assessment in the United States.

Another performance assessment developed and used in U.S. higher education came from Educational Testing Service (ETS). To assess non-native speakers' English proficiency for study in North American universities, ETS developed two performance-style tests—the TSE® (Test of Spoken English) and the TWE® (Test of Written English). Although these tests no longer exist, they both have been incorporated into revised versions of the TOEFL® iBT.

In the classroom, the enthusiasm for performance assessment in language education has been sustained by its alignment with approaches to language teaching such as task-based instruction, content-based instruction, and the communicative approach. Cross-country initiatives such as the Common European Framework of Reference (CERF), another scale used to describe language (Council of Europe, 2011), have generated continued focus on performance assessment. CERF was developed as a common reference for teaching, learning, and assessment of foreign language learning across Europe.

Performance assessment is popular with teachers and learners because it seems more authentic than other kinds of tests. Language use situations, particularly those involving oral and written communication, usually require the production of language to complete some purpose. Performance assessment allows test developers to create tasks that require production for an authentic purpose.

Certainly performance assessment is a valuable approach to testing language ability, and in many cases, it is the best option. However, there are limitations to this approach, and strategic planning is needed to accurately assess performances. Research has focused on two important issues: scoring performances and transferring assessment performances to authentic situations.

What's the Score?

Most tests eventually boil down to a score as a number or a level. For performance assessment, generating a score can be the point where an assessment loses credibility or accuracy. As Cohen (1994) says, "The important point is that the scores themselves are arbitrary. The main concern is interpretation of the scores. A score has meaning only in terms of some point of reference" (p. 98). Developing or selecting a scale is a challenge teachers face because many possibilities exist for language performance.

Transforming a performance into a score is usually done by a rater or teacher using one of these rating scales (see Figure 3.3) or a rubric. During the rating process, many challenges occur that must be considered to ensure consistency in a performance test. This consistency, known as **reliability**, provides a level of assurance that scores truly reflect test-takers' language ability and are not the result of error or

FIGURE 3.3: Three Common Rating Scale Structures

Holistic: Holistic scales ask raters to consider each test-taker's performance in a unified way. Scales may include descriptors for different features, but these are not rated separately. The score represents an overall general level for the performance.

Example of a three-level holistic writing scale:

Level	Description
1	Clarity lacking due to grammar and vocabulary issues. Limited development (one to four sentences).
2	Understandable but without detail. Shows some control of grammar but limited in complex use of language. Ideas are organized.
3	Ideas presented in a clear and developed manner. Writing is easy to read and includes specific details as well as some complex vocabulary and sentence structures.

Analytic: Analytic scales divide a performance into aspects and give a separate score for each aspect. These separate scores are usually totaled for a final score, which makes the weighting of each area very important.

Example of an analytic scale for writing assessment:

Organization: Introduction, conclusion, thesis, paragraphing, coherence
      Points: 1   2   3   4   5

Development: Appropriate length, support of main point, examples used, completeness
      Points: 1   2   3   4   5

Accurate language use: Accurate grammar and sentence structure, correct word choices
      Points: 1   2   3   4   5

Complex language use: Variety in sentence complexity, precise word use
      Points: 1   2   3   4   5

Primary trait: Primary trait scales are similar to analytic scales; they are also divided into aspects of performance. However, with a primary trait scale, a checklist approach is used to determine if the performance has certain specific features. The scale lists the desired features, and raters look for evidence for each of them.

Example of a primary trait scale for writing assessment:

1. Clear thesis statement	Yes	No
2. Logical organization	Yes	No
3. Introduction to engage reader	Yes	No
4. At least two main ideas in body	Yes	No
5. Appropriate support for main ideas	Yes	No
6. Grammatical accuracy at least 90%	Yes	No
7. Vocabulary used correctly at least 85%	Yes	No
8. Sentence structures are varied	Yes	No

randomness. Research has illuminated potential issues with the rating process in performance assessments.

Knoch (2009) compared two different rating scales used to assess writing. The first was a standard analytic composition scale focused on writing issues such as organization, development, and language use. The other scale was data-driven; it was generated from actual writing samples from the test (see Figure 3.4 on rating scale development). The data-driven scale was based on 600 diagnostic writing samples and, rather than general descriptors for each feature, it included specific measures such as error-free sentences. In the study, the two scales were used to rate a writing assessment for undergraduate students. Ten raters marked 100 essays using both scales in rating sessions two months apart. After comparing the ratings, Knoch determined that the data-driven scale was better at discriminating writing proficiencies; there was also more agreement among raters and more consistent ratings. This scale was easier and quicker for raters to learn and provided more concrete information to test-takers as well. Knoch's findings indicated that the empirical data-driven scale had more validity and reliability. This research shows how the type of scale used may affect the accuracy of performance scoring.

FIGURE 3.4: Rating Scale Development Approaches: Definitions

Theory Based: Scales that try to capture the underlying construct of language ability by using a theoretical model to create descriptors and categories for a rating scale.

Practice Based: In educational contexts, rating scales are often developed to reflect the curriculum or lessons from a course. They may also be based on the input of educators familiar with the students and the assessment setting.

Data Driven: Scales may be developed using sample or actual performances from a performance assessment. Generally, a sample set of performances is collected and analyzed for salient features at different proficiency levels.

Once a scale or rubric has been chosen, adopted, or developed to assess performances, the issue arises as to how consistently teachers or raters use it. Lumely (2005) explains that "the scale takes no action of its own, and remains lifeless and unrelated to language performances until used by a rater" (p. 239). In non-classroom testing, such as placement or proficiency tests, raters are trained and retrained to make sure they are rating consistently. Teachers often do not have the advantage of such training before using a scale, which may lead to problems with how they use it. However, research has shown that even when they agree on scores, raters may not be considering the same aspects of language in their decisions. Lumely (2002) also conducted a study about raters and assessment criteria. He looked at the process that raters using an analytical scale followed in scoring 24 ESL writing tests. During the rating session, they were asked to follow a think-aloud protocol in which they vocalized any thoughts that came to mind while completing their ratings. Lumely found that the raters overall paid attention to the rating scale uniformly and used all the descriptors, but he identified a variety of strategies used by raters to deal with challenges in arriving at a final score. For example, when trying to rate a performance that fell on the boundary between two scoring categories, some raters compared the performance with other performances or tried to expand or narrow the scope of a scoring category to justify their decision. Lumely (2005) explains that rating is "fundamentally a social procedure organized around the need to bring intuitive reactions into conformity with the requirements of the testing institution" (p. 240). This research indicates that even with a well-developed rating scale, raters' application of that scale may vary. For teachers without such training, this issue is also a challenge; they may not be using the scale in the same way for each student in their class.

With evidence that raters vary in their interpretation and use of rating scales, researchers have looked at what may be causing this variance. One factor is whether the rater is a native or non-native speaker of the language being tested (Brown, 1995; Chalhoub-Deville, 1995; Hamp-Lyons & Zhang, 2001; Hill, 1996; Zhang & Elder, 2011). These studies have conflicting results, perhaps due to different performance assessment tasks, different data collection and analyses, and a variety of rating scales. This distinction between native and non-native speakers is problematic as it is not a straightforward or even an accurate dichotomy. Some studies claim that non-native speakers are harsher when rating performances (Fayer & Krasinski, 1987). Others have shown them to be more lenient (Hill, 1996), while still others have observed little difference between the two groups (Brown, 1995; Hamp-Lyons & Zhang, 2001; Kim, 2009).

In a study that illustrates these mixed findings, Zhang and Elder (2011) studied the oral proficiency ratings on the College English Test–Spoken English Test (CET–SET) given in China. They collected holistic ratings on 30 speaking tests from 19 native-English and 20 non-native English speakers as well as written comments by the raters. Using both quantitative and qualitative analyses, they determined that both groups were similar in their holistic ratings and the components of speaking to which they attended. Differences emerged, however, in how the two groups of raters weighted aspects of speaking; for example, the non-native raters commented more on the linguistic ability of the speakers, while the natives were more attentive to communicative strategies and interaction.

Other characteristics of raters have been studied, such as second language proficiency and teaching or rating experience (Lim, 2011; Weigle, 1994, 1998; Winke, Gass, & Myford, 2013) to see how these individual differences affect scores. Barkaoui (2011) looked at 31 novice and 29 experienced raters of ESL compositions, using two kinds of rating scales, analytic and holistic. He found that the analytic scale distinguished writing ability more precisely. In comparing the two groups of raters over time, the experienced raters had better *inter*-rater reliability (they were more likely to agree with other raters) and *intra*-rater reliability (more consistent themselves in their ratings). The experienced raters were also found less likely to use the full range of the scales, which may have resulted in their consistency. Both groups of raters had more self-consistency with the analytic scale. Having details provided for each of the criteria seemed to guide these raters, perhaps showing that rubrics are easier to use than scales. Barkaoui's study shows the complicated interplay between rating scale types and raters' backgrounds. Indeed, performance assessment scores are affected both by who the raters are and how they rate.

Authenticity: Transferring a Performance to the Real World

While it seems obvious that an oral interview provides more authentic use of spoken language than answering multiple choice questions, scholars have questioned the assumption that performing for an assessment produces a sample of authentic language. The premise that performance on a test is transferrable to actual language use has some underlying complexities. Some researchers have pointed out that tasks in real-life settings may be impossible to create in testing situations. For example, writing a biology lab report is an authentic academic task; however, it would not work well in an assessment because of physical and time constraints—test-takers cannot conduct a science experiment and then write about it during a test. At the same time, if such test tasks are not authentic, it can affect both the reliability and validity of the test. Therefore, authenticity still requires systematic attention when creating tasks for language testing and learning.

For example, researchers have critiqued oral interviews for their assumed authenticity. Use of the Oral Proficiency Interview (OPI) with the ACTFL Guidelines has been advocated in part because of its proximity to real-life tasks, such as conversational interaction (Liskin-Gasparro, 2003). However, Raffaldini (1988) argues that the OPI is not a conversation since the context does not encourage a natural give-and-take between the interviewer and the test-taker. He claims the imbalance between the test-taker and interviewer is problematic because of how questions are initiated by the interviewer. Question formation is a frequent and difficult conversational gambit English language learners must develop, but it is usually not tested in the interview format.

Another example is from a study by Leki and Carson (1997), which compared actual university academic writing with the writing tasks students were given in their academically oriented English language classes. They interviewed 27 ESL students in the U.S. who reported that they were asked to write from source material in their academic classes, while they primarily wrote essays without using other texts in the English language classes. One student's comment, which was chosen as the title for the article, was that the writing required in these two settings was from "completely different worlds." Students mentioned other differences between the academically oriented ESL classes and actual academic classwork beyond source use and linguistic issues: among them were audience, rhetorical style, and emphasis on content. The research surrounding the authenticity of oral interviews (Bachman, 1988; Bachman & Savignon, 1986; Fulcher, 1996) and independent essays emphasizes that before assuming the authenticity of a performance assessment, we need to analyze both the task that we are trying to simulate and the interactions elicited.

What We Can Do . . .

While research has shown that certain aspects of performance assessment can be challenging, teachers can minimize these problems through (1) careful development and evaluation of test tasks and (2) thoughtful planning and monitoring of the rating/scoring procedures. With attention to these two aspects, performance assessment can be a valuable method to assess students' language use.

1. Develop authentic assessment tasks.

The issue of authenticity can be managed by using a careful needs analysis and piloting tasks beforehand. Performance assessments in language classes are usually tasks such as making a presentation, writing a paragraph or essay, or giving extended, unrehearsed answers to questions. These tasks are more motivating and useful when they reflect language students will need when undertaking future communicative situations. Carefully considering these potential uses can help ensure that this connection is strong.

One approach is to conduct a **needs analysis**, which is part of curriculum development, but on a smaller scale, which can also inform task development for performance assessment. For example, before assigning an academic writing assessment task, teachers can ask students to collect samples of writing assignments from courses in their disciplines, such as Engineering, Biology, or Psychology. Finding some common elements among authentic assignments can be a starting place for task development. Another possibility is to talk with professors or scholars in a variety of academic fields to identify common writing tasks and the characteristics or criteria for effective writing in their fields. A number of studies characterizing academic writing (Carson, 2001; Horowitz, 1986; Leki & Carson, 1994, 1997) could be considered as teachers develop tasks.

A checklist can help pinpoint aspects of real-world tasks to include in performance assessment. Perfect alignment is nearly impossible; however, systematically checking the similarities between the task and the real situation helps us to account for differences (Bachman & Palmer, 1996). Some areas to consider when comparing real-world and test tasks are:

- What is the setting?
- Is there any time for preparation beforehand?
- What is the length of the discourse?
- Who is involved? One, two, or more people?
- Is there much interaction? If so, what are the different roles for the participants?
- What are some typical responses?
- For this task, what makes a performance successful?

Even when tasks have been developed that we think are authentic, interesting, and useful, it is hard to guarantee that they will work the way we planned. For this reason, it is important to try out the performance task by asking someone to complete it while you observe. This rehearsal helps to determine adequate timing, clarity of instruction, and usefulness of the rating rubric. For higher-stakes assessments, such as placement testing, teachers can evaluate how students complete the task by collecting data via observations, think-aloud protocols, follow-up interviews, or short questionnaires. Several pilot sessions could be completed to get input from various perspectives: high- and low-proficiency learners, teachers/students, and raters. Trying out and piloting informs task development and can help with revision as well as provide evidence of authenticity.

2. Select or develop good rubrics and critique them for your context.

When planning an assessment, selecting or developing a rubric or scale is an important step to take long before the task is given to actual students. For classroom purposes, a rubric may be a better choice than a scale if it provides more detail for students and teachers. (See Figure 3.5 for a sample rubric.) In many cases, adopting a rubric that has been developed by someone else is perfectly acceptable. Rubrics are widely available through teachers' manuals, online resources, or from research studies. However, choosing a rubric should be done with several considerations in mind:

- Does the rubric reflect the goals of your course, including the curriculum, lessons, assignments, and grading on previous assignments?
- Does it align with your sense of what language use is? If the scale or rubric is analytic (see Figure 3.3), then be sure that the points for each criterion reflect the weighting of skills in the classroom. It should also reflect the purpose of the assessment.
- Does the rubric fit the task? A clear match should exist between the instructions on the task and the rubric, and some assurance that the language produced from the task can be evaluated using the descriptors.
- Does the scoring scheme fit students? The example from the In the Real World story shows the problems that can arise when the level of proficiency does not align with the rubric. Will the highest-proficiency students be able to get a high score? Will it appropriately distinguish the ability levels of students? This last question might go beyond the descriptors in the rubric to the point system used for scoring.

All of these questions should be addressed before an assessment is adopted. However, evaluation of a rubric's success should be revisited soon after it is used the first time to determine if it worked well or if it should be revised before it is used again.

Another option is to develop a new scale or rubric. Several approaches to this have already been discussed (see Figure 3.4 on rating scale development). In developing a rubric for a classroom test, you might start by combining your experience with and knowledge of the students in your class with your definition of language use. Also, looking at the assignments, lessons, and curriculum may help identify key components for your scale.

Another possibility is to review student performances on an assessment task and divide them into levels for a data-driven scale. The levels should then be scrutinized to consider what aspects of language distinguish them. Working with a team of teachers might ensure more diverse opinions and reduce bias. Then the aspects that differentiate the samples can be molded into a rubric or scales. This data-driven approach should be checked for alignment with the course to avoid rating students on language features with which they have not had instruction or experience. For larger-scale tests, such as placement or proficiency testing, this approach has been found to create highly reliable scales (Knoch, 2009), and if teachers are involved in the development process, the impact on the classroom and attitudes about testing may improve (Plakans, 2013; Turner & Upshur, 1996, 2002).

3. Prepare for scoring.

In classroom assessment, the rater is usually the teacher, which may create some challenges for rating performances but may also be beneficial. Teachers are more sensitive to problems in rating scales because they know more about their students' abilities than a single performance can capture. This sensitivity can help identify problems in a scale. However, the subjectivity that can affect rating sometimes concerns teachers because impressions of students can unintentionally bleed into their ratings. Ideally, a solid rubric protects against unintentional

FIGURE 3.5: Sample Rubric for a Research Report Assignment, with Annotation

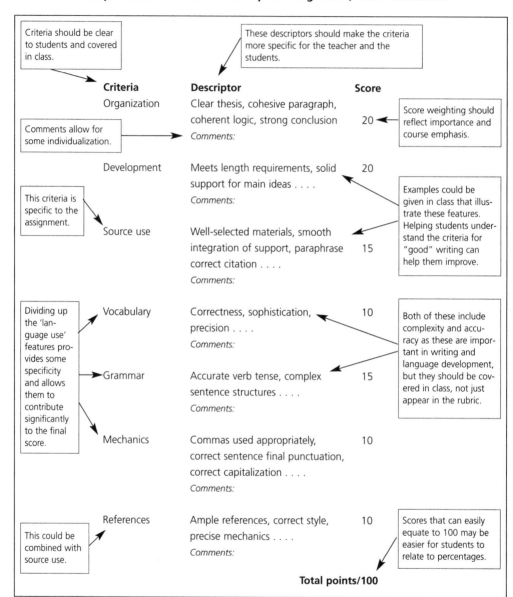

bias. Figure 3.5 shows several key features that can improve the trust-worthiness of a rubric for both students and teachers.

Several other precautions can ensure that the rating process is fair to students. For writing assessment, students' names can be removed from the performance; instead an ID number or some other identifier can conceal their identities from the rater. Another option is to have a co-rater, such as a colleague who teaches a similar course, also rate performances or a portion of them just to check that the teacher is on the right track. An extreme measure is to have the performances rated by someone other than the teacher. For classroom assessment, however, this might exclude the advantages knowledgeable teachers have in rating situations because it takes the performance out of context.

In some testing situations, teachers are not the raters. In these cases, time should be devoted to training raters, and, once a test is in use, raters should have regular brush-up sessions to make sure they are still rating accurately. These sessions should include shared listening to/reading samples and discussion of rating scales, exposure to several performances at each level of the rating scale, practice rating with group discussion, and practice rating individually with feedback from the trainer. Rater training should be taken seriously and requires intensive discussion. It is impossible to eliminate the subjectivity of judging performances; however, rater training minimizes it to some degree. Over time, raters will need to train on scoring as ratings can become intuitive and possibly drift away from the descriptors on the scale. A short brush-up session can bring raters back to the rubric and allow them to check their own performance.

4

Multiple choice tests are inaccurate measures of language but are easy to write.

In the Real World . . .

At the time this book was written, I had a student named Matthew who was pursuing a degree at the American University in Cairo. (This is Atta.) Before joining the MA TESOL program, Matthew had no formal teacher training except for a one-month intensive TEFL course from a non-accredited training center. Before going to Egypt, he taught in a U.S. public school as a part-time teacher and in Asia as a full-time teacher. As a graduate student, he had a job as a teaching fellow in a foundational ESL program that prepares students for their academic study in an Egyptian university where English is the language of instruction. During this experience, Matthew taught courses in study skills, grammar, and vocabulary for both graduate and undergraduate students.

As part of his MA TESOL program, he took an introductory language assessment course with me. For the first time, Matthew received formal training in developing multiple choice question (MCQ) items.

In the following passage, he reflects on his changing attitude toward MCQs:

We have all heard students complain about tests: tricky questions, unclear questions, questions that are too hard, and more. Many of us have probably had those same feelings when we were students. And this might be particularly true with multiple choice questions (MCQs). As a student, did you ever find yourself thinking: "There are two right answers to this question" or "What trick is the teacher trying to play on me with this question?" If you did, you are not alone.

That being said, I might be an unusual case. Not only have I always generally liked MCQ items, both as an instructor and as a student, but I have also rarely heard my students complain about my MCQ items. This might seem like an ideal situation, but it created a problem in that I just kind of uncritically assumed that my MCQ items were good. I did not critique or evaluate the purpose or quality of MCQs closely enough. I assumed that MCQs worked well in "most situations," and I assumed that most MCQs that I wrote were achieving what I had hoped they would achieve.

Now, I pause here because, like me, you probably do write good MCQs much of the time. Most of the MCQs that I wrote generally did achieve what I intended. But such success was either by luck or intuition at best. And while intuition plays an important part in developing test items, it alone is not sufficient.

After taking an assessment course, I went back and evaluated some of my MCQs using some of the skills that I gained from the course. I realized that a number of my questions were not nearly as strong as I had believed. I was saddened to discover some questions were quite poor in differentiating between the high- and low-performing students. I found other items that almost everyone missed or almost everyone got correct. Such items provided virtually no assessment value.

In hindsight, I no longer just assume that MCQs are inherently good or bad. MCQs can indeed be a great tool in the assessment toolbox; I use them often. But now I have learned to write better items—items that better differentiate students, and items that are really testing what I want them to test. As it is, assessments already create enough stress and work for students and instructors alike; there is no need to complicate the situation with poorly written items.

Matthew's narrative includes insightful comments about MCQs. Many teachers like MCQs because they appear easy to write. Matthew made reference to this, but he also came to understand the complex nature of MCQs. Many of the concerns teachers voice about MCQ tests are actually related to the quality of item writing rather than to question format. Teachers may not receive training in writing items and consequently may craft problematic test questions.

What the Research Says . . .

Many of the negative associations with MCQs are likely due to their longstanding relationship with externally mandated standardized testing. The United States is known for its emphasis on standardized exams that frequently include objective items like multiple choice questions. We often hear teachers and students expressing dissatisfaction that MCQs are neither able to adequately capture language use nor appear authentic; these are common complaints about MCQs used in school settings.

One major concern with MCQ tests focuses on validity. Critics argue that interpretations and inferences based on MCQ scores are not accurate because MCQs lack authenticity. According to this view, MCQs do not adequately simulate how language is used in real life. While this is partially true, we cannot ignore the fact that MCQs sometimes provide better coverage of content than, for example, performance-based assessments. Because of their unique format, MCQs offer test developers the chance to test students across the breadth of course content. This representative sample can provide content-related validity evidence. It can also help avoid **construct underrepresentation** (Messick, 1989), a concept that relates to inadequate content coverage. For example, an essay exam that asks students to write three or four paragraphs on one given topic can limit the performance of test-takers, especially if that topic is one about which they have little knowledge. However, a 50-item MCQ test can allow the test-takers to reveal what they know about a wide range of topics. Although scholars have argued that content-related validity evidence is not sufficient to ensure score validity, it has substantial importance in test validation, especially in achievement testing (Kane, 2006). (Myth 6 discusses validity in greater detail.)

The comparison between MCQ and direct tests (such as writing and speaking exams or performance assessment) is another issue related to validity. As shown in Myth 3, there is controversy as to whether performance assessment provides better information about students' abilities. However, a meta-analysis conducted by Rodriguez (2003) showed that selected-response items (such as MCQs) and constructed-response items (such as writing tasks) were highly correlated when developed to test the same concept. In other words, both testing formats yielded similar scores when administered to test-takers. Research (Gebril, 2009, 2010) has also shown that MCQs have much higher score reliability than performance assessment, which has often had relatively low score reliability for reasons mentioned in Myth 3.

The higher score reliability of MCQs is the result of a number of factors. First, these MCQ tests usually include a large number of items, something that always contributes to score reliability. In addition, scoring of MCQs is objective since human judgment is usually not an issue as it is with performance assessment where raters are making the decisions. Scoring multiple choice questions is easier for teachers because of their objectivity. These facts about MCQs minimize the error in test scores and, by default, enhance the accuracy of test results.

Another criticism of MCQs is that students can score well by simply guessing. This is true, but critics tend to ignore a number of other issues. First, the effects of guessing are minimized if MCQs are well written. By carefully crafting MCQs, we can avoid giving unintended clues to test-takers. Also, guessing can be controlled by increasing the number of answer options in MCQs. For example, when three options are offered, the guessing probability will be 33 percent. However, when the options are increased to four or five, the probability of guessing right decreases to 25 percent and 20 percent, respectively. Downing (2006) refers to the extremely low probability of obtaining a high score on a test based on random guessing. He reports that the statistical probability of a test-taker obtaining 70 percent on a three-option, 30-item test by randomly guessing is 0.0000356. Also, he indicates that the probability of getting two of three-option items right based on random guessing is 0.11, getting three items correct is 0.04, getting four items is 0.01, and getting five items is 0.004. Based on this information, we can conclude that random guessing should not be a huge concern in MCQ tests.

More important, the use of recent statistical techniques controls for guessing during the scoring of standardized tests. For example, item response theory (IRT) provides mathematical procedures that account for guessing effects. While such analyses may not be used very often in classroom assessment, they increase confidence in results from larger-scale language tests that use MCQs.

What We Can Do . . .

While the criticisms directed toward MCQ tests are plausible, a number of procedures can help teachers avoid many of these problematic issues in developing tests.

1. Plan what you want your test to test.

Planning time will vary depending on the scale of the test development project; however, regardless of the size of the project, you need to plan carefully before starting this process. Identifying the needs and resources (both human and physical) before developing an MCQ test is very important. Planning involves coming up with answers for a wide range of questions related to test development, and actually many of the questions listed are relevant to any test format, not just MCQ tests.

QUESTIONS IN PLANNING TESTS

- What is the purpose of this test? What decisions will be made based on test scores?
- What is the test construct? In other words, what are the language skills or features to be assessed by this test?
- Who are the item writers? Are you going to write the items yourself? Or will you hire other people to write them for you?
- What quality assurance procedures will you use to check the validity and reliability of your test questions?
- What other human resources are needed in addition to writers? Do you need administrative assistance? Information technology specialists? Item moderators (reviewers)? Proctors?
- What physical resources are needed? A photocopier to prepare copies of your test? Special paper, such as bubble sheets? A computer lab?
- Where will you administer the test? Are the testing rooms well equipped?
- Are you going to use machines or humans for scoring?
- How are you going to report the results to your students?

2. Establish clear test specifications.

Once the language skills and elements of interest in the assessment are identified, teachers should determine the content of the MCQs. An effective strategy is to develop some test specifications, usually in a table format. Test specifications serve as a roadmap or a blueprint for a test and usually include these sections:

- general description of the test content
- language skills/elements assessed
- sub-skills or areas assessed under each language skill/element

- number of questions/items targeting each skill
- number of options for answering each MCQ
- weight for each question/section
- time needed for each section
- a description of the expected length, genre, topic, and linguistic complexity of the text if the MCQ will be based on a reading or listening text

Preparing test specifications serves several purposes in the test development process with these functions and benefits:

- They provide guidance for test developers in planning the item-writing process ahead of time.
- They guide writers during test development.
- They guide reviewers when critiquing items.
- They provide validity evidence for the test (showing whether the content is representative of the language domain being assessed).
- They provide information for teachers as well as students who are preparing for the test.
- They provide information to other stakeholders including administrators, policymakers, and test users who might need to make decisions about a test for a specific context.

Tables 4.1 and 4.2 provide examples of test specifications for the MCQ section of a reading test. Reading tests usually offer a number of passages with subsequent questions targeting information in these passages. Table 4.1 shows information for a reading passage of a test, and Table 4.2 includes specifications for the MCQs for this passage. In these MCQs, the test developer is targeting a number of reading sub-skills such as skimming, scanning, making inferences, and guessing the meaning of certain words based on the context. Table 4.2 also specifies the number of MCQs targeting each of these sub-skills and the number of options each MCQ should include. Finally, the table provides the

TABLE 4.1: Example of Specifications for a Reading Passage

Length	300 words
Topics	General
Range of vocabulary	Familiar/non-technical
Range of structures	Structures are not complex; suitable for intermediate students
Readability / difficulty level	Moderate difficulty
Style	Formal
Genre	Magazine/newspaper articles

TABLE 4.2: Example of a Simple Reading Task Specifications Table

Skills	Question Format	# of Questions	Weight	Points
Skimming	MCQ (4 options)	2	20%	5 each
Scanning	MCQ (4 options)	4	40%	5 each
Making inferences	MCQ (4 options)	2	20%	5 each
Guessing meaning based on context	MCQ (4 options)	2	20%	5 each
				TOTAL: 50 points

suggested weight for each sub-skill. Clearly, these specifications do not leave any room for unnecessary creativity on the part of writers. By using such a scheme, we can ensure that if we have multiple writers, they will develop relatively similar and consistently uniform test questions based on the same specifications.

3. Write effective multiple choice questions.

Although a number of questions related to format should be considered before writing any MCQs, let's first look at the basic anatomy of a MCQ item. The example in Figure 4.1 includes four main parts: the

FIGURE 4.1: Anatomy of an MCQ Item

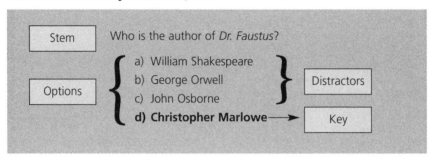

stem, the options, the distractors, and the key. The **stem** precedes the options; in the example, it asks the question about the author of the play *Dr. Faustus*. Next, the four options provide answers from which test-takers choose. Usually only one is the correct answer, the **key**; the others, called **distractors**, are incorrect.

To write effectively, some guidelines about the parts of a MCQ are useful (Downing, 2006, p. 294):

- Minimize the amount of reading in each item.
- Ensure that the question stem is very clear.
- Include the central idea in the stem, not in the options.
- Word the stem positively; avoid negatives such as *not* or *except*. If negative words are required in the stem, use them cautiously and ensure that they are capitalized and in bold type (e.g., **NOT** or **NEVER**) so that students will be less likely to miss the negation.

To minimize guessing, the recommended number of options for each MCQ is four, although some people argue that five are even better. However, coming up with plausible and defensible distractors is a hard task, and, for this reason, writing a good five-option item is difficult. Since research has shown that random guessing has little effect on test scores, if writing four or five good choices is not possible, then three options may still be safe.

If you have written MCQs, then you know that creating options or distractors is the most challenging part of the process. To write effective options, these guidelines (adapted from Downing, 2006, p. 294) can be helpful:

- Develop as many effective choices as you can, but three are adequate.
- Make sure that only one of these choices can be the correct answer.
- Vary the location of the correct answer according to the number of choices.
- Balance the answer key, as much as possible, so that the correct answer appears an equal number of times (or close to it) in each answer position.
- Keep choices independent; they should not overlap in meaning.
- Keep choices similar and parallel in content and grammatical structure.
- Keep the length of choices about equal, if possible.
- *None of the above* should be used sparingly.
- *All of the above* should be avoided as it can change the difficulty of the question dramatically.
- Make all distractors plausible (not obviously impossible).
- Avoid giving clues to the right answer, such as:
  a. specific determiners, including *always, never, completely,* and *absolutely.*
  b. **clang associations,** choices identical to or resembling words in the stem.
  c. grammatical inconsistencies that cue the test-taker to the correct choice.
  d. a conspicuously correct choice.
  e. pairs or triplets of options that clue the test-taker to the correct choice.
  f. blatantly absurd, ridiculous options.

To illustrate some potential challenges in writing MCQs, Figure 4.2 provides examples of problematic MCQ items in the left column and a revised version of these items in the right. Item 1 has a redundancy problem because the phrase *Adam went to Chicago* is repeated. The revised item removes this phrase from the options and includes it in the stem, minimizing the reading load and reducing redundancy. Item 2 has an overlapping problem; the first option, *University education,* can subsume the other three. Also, the second option, *Graduate degree,* includes two of the options: *Master of Arts* and *PhD in Education.* The revised draft on the right replaces the two overlapping options with two new ones. In Item 3, the indefinite article *an* provides an unintended clue since test-takers can immediately discard options b and c, which start with consonants, without knowing the correct answer. The revised draft solves this problem by including indefinite articles in all of the options.

FIGURE 4.2: Examples of Revised MCQ Items

Problematic Item	Better Item

1. Why did Adam go to Chicago?
  a. Adam went to Chicago to see his friends.
  b. Adam went to Chicago to visit his parents.
  c. Adam went to Chicago to watch the game.
	1. Adam went to Chicago to . . .
	  a. see his friends.
	
	  b. visit his parents.
	
	  c. watch the game.

2. What academic qualifications are needed for this job?
  a. University education
  b. Graduate degree
  c. Master of Arts
  d. PhD in Education
	2. What academic qualifications are needed for this job?
	  a. Master of Arts
	  b. Diploma in education
	  c. Teaching certificate
	  d. Only a bachelor's degree

3. According to the passage, John works as an
  a. engineer.
  b. novelist.
  c. chemist.
  d. astronomer.
	3. According to the passage, John works as
	  a. an engineer.
	  b. a novelist.
	  c. a chemist.
	  d. an astronomer.

4. Ruthlessly critique your items.

Once you have finished writing MCQs, it is always a good idea to solicit feedback on the questions from other colleagues. Item critiquing is important because it is hard to identify problems in our own test writing. It is dangerous to think that your items are perfect and not seek feedback from colleagues. Items can usually be improved by being scrutinized and through feedback. But for a successful item evaluation process, some guidelines for item review are needed. A copy of the test specifications will help item reviewers identify the sub-skill/content area to be tested by each MCQ and consider whether they have been successfully transformed into actual items. Reviewers can also look at the clarity of the instructions, the accuracy of the language used in the items, and issues pertaining to the quality of the items themselves. Figure 4.3 lists important issues for MCQ review.

FIGURE 4.3: Guidelines for Reviewing MCQ Items

MCQ Test Instructions/Directions
❑ Are the instructions clear? Is there any ambiguity?
❑ Are the instructions sufficient?
❑ Are the instructions placed where they are needed?

Language Used in the MCQ Item
❑ Is it grammatically correct?
❑ Is it clear? Could test-takers understand this item differently than you intend?
❑ Is the language concise? Could it convey the message successfully with fewer words?

Item Quality
❑ Is the stem effective?
❑ Is only one answer correct (the key)?
❑ Are the distractors plausible?
❑ Are the options almost the same length?
❑ Do either the stem or the options provide any unintended clues?

---

5. Pilot multiple choice questions.

After writing and reviewing items, it is always a good idea to pilot them with a group similar to the population for which the test has been developed, particularly for large-scale tests. The purpose of piloting is to check whether the items and the test are appropriate for this test-taking population. This information is usually collected from piloting:

1. clarity of instructions (items are free from ambiguity)
2. clarity of language used in the test items (so that test-takers will interpret the language used in the items precisely)
3. cultural appropriateness of test items
4. item statistics (item difficulty and item discrimination will be discussed in the next section)
5. test reliability

Information about the first three of these points can be obtained qualitatively during piloting. Ask about five people to take the test, and then informally inquire about the clarity of the language used in the instructions and the items. If descriptive statistics (item difficulty and discrimination) and test reliability are of interest, more test-takers will be needed. To obtain stable estimates of these statistics, Fulcher (2010) believes that at least 30 test-takers are needed for piloting, and even more in the context of large-scale assessment.

6. Analyze test items for difficulty and discrimination statistics.

After collecting pilot data, the results can be used to calculate statistics, in particular, item difficulty and item discrimination. In many cases, such as in placement testing, MCQ tests include items of varying difficulty levels that target the proficiency levels of test-takers. For example, in an ESL reading placement test, the questions must challenge a range of ability levels from beginning to advanced. If the questions are all at the same level, the test is not measuring across the range of difficulty, and the resulting scores will not be useful in placing students into the appropriate classes.

While experienced item writers and reviewers can usually pitch MCQ items to the right level, we cannot be sure without calculating item difficulty. As mentioned earlier, this information can be obtained based on the results of piloting. The calculation of item difficulty is fairly straightforward: Identify how many test-takers answered the item correctly out of the total number as in this formula:

Item difficulty = # of test-takers who selected the right answer / total number of test-takers

For example, if 40 out of 50 students who answered a multiple choice question selected the correct answer, we get this:

Item difficulty = 40/50 = 0.8

In this example, the item difficulty is 0.8 since 80 percent of the students got the item right. Item difficulty values ranges from 0–1; when the value gets higher, the item becomes less difficult or easier. Item difficulty values ranging from 0.1–0.3 tend to be associated with difficult items, while values ranging from 0.8–1.0 indicate an easy item. (If 100 percent of the test-takers got the correct answer, it would have the value 1.)

Item discrimination means that a specific item has the ability to distinguish between high- and low-proficiency students. Generally, we expect students with advanced language proficiency to perform better on an item than low-proficiency students. When weaker students perform better than stronger students, that item is said to have poor discrimination ability or low item discrimination. A number of procedures can be used to calculate item discrimination; one simple one is described here, but readers who are interested in more sophisticated techniques for calculating discrimination should consult Bachman (2004).

Since the purpose of item discrimination is to compare the performance of both high- and low-proficiency test-takers, these groups need to be determined, and their total scores on the test can serve this purpose. For example, after obtaining the total scores of 100 test-takers who took a certain exam, a cut-off point for each group should be determined to identify the high- and low-scoring examinees. You can identify the highest scoring 25 percent of the test-takers (high-scoring group) and then the lowest-scoring 25 percent of the same group (low-scoring group) by ranking those students from 1–100, from highest to lowest (the highest and lowest 27% or 33% is another option). Next, determine how many students in each group got the item correct. This information determines item difficulty. To obtain item discrimination using this simple technique, first calculate item difficulty.

Table 4.3 shows examples of item difficulty information for both the low-scoring (N=25) group (LSG) and high-scoring (N=25) group (HSG) on an MCQ item. Remember that we are working here at the item level, not the total score obtained on the test. The total score for a specific student is used to place him or her into the high- or low-scoring group. Analysis is then conducted for each question separately. As described in Table 4.3, 20 students from the high-scoring group got the item correct, while only 10 students from the low-scoring group answered it correctly. Using the formula introduced in the previous section, item difficulty for both groups is calculated (see Table 4.3).

TABLE 4.3: Example of MCQ Analysis, Item Difficulty

Group	# of Students Who Got the Item Correct	# of Students Who Got the Item Wrong	Item Difficulty
High-scoring (HSG) N=25	20	5	0.8
Low-scoring (LSG) N=25	10	15	0.4

To investigate how well this item was able to discriminate between stronger and weaker test-takers, we need to use the item difficulty values for both groups. Item discrimination will be calculated as follows:

Item discrimination = (# correct for HSG / total # HSG)–
$$(\text{\# correct for LSG / total \# LSG})$$
$$= (20/25) - (10/25)$$
$$= 0.8 - 0.4 \text{ (i.e., item difficulty for HSG - item difficulty of LSQ)}$$
$$= 0.4$$

After calculating item discrimination, how can different item-discrimination values be interpreted? The item discrimination index (D) ranges from 1 to –1; negative values usually occur when the number of low-scoring students who answered a specific MCQ correctly exceeds the number of the high-scoring students.

According to Table 4.4, any item discrimination value above 0.3 is acceptable and indicates good discrimination ability. However, any value below 0.3 should be interpreted in the light of item-difficulty values since item discrimination is affected by the difficulty level of an item. Very easy or very difficult items usually have low discrimination values, and for this reason, item difficulty must be examined before assessing item discrimination. As shown in Table 4.4, if an item has a discrimination value between 0.2 and 0.3, this is acceptable if the item is difficult/easy (i.e., has either a high- or low-item difficulty value), but such items do not provide a lot of information about test-takers. When an item is answered correctly by 99 percent of test-takers, it does not provide any useful information and consequently does not discriminate well among the examinees. However, if the item is of medium difficulty (around 0.5), this is the ideal situation for obtaining good discrimination values. When an item with medium difficulty has a discrimination value below 0.3, this item should be checked and revised. Items between 0 and 0.2, especially for those with medium difficulty, must be checked carefully for the reasons mentioned earlier: any negative discrimination value indicates a serious flaw. This item should either be removed or completely revised.

TABLE 4.4: Interpreting Item Discrimination at Different Difficulty Levels

	For Difficult Items	For Items of Medium Difficulty	For Easy Items
Item Discrimination	Action Needed		
0.3 or above	Accept	Accept	Accept
0.2–0.3	Accept	Revise	Accept
0–0.2	May need revising	Revise	May need revising
Negative value	Revise or remove	Revise or remove	Revise or remove

7. Take advantage of test accommodation strategies when needed.

Although MCQs are practical and easy to administer, some groups of test-takers might find them challenging. For example, if we are administering a listening test to a group of young learners whose language proficiency is relatively low, it is a good idea to make some changes to minimize the reading load in items. If we are not testing reading, the limited reading ability of these learners should not affect their performance on the test (this refers to *accommodations*, a term defined in Myth 1).

Figure 4.4 shows an example of an MCQ with pictorial options for your English learners, which is not typical of most exams where the options are presented through written statements. Instead test-takers have to choose the right picture. As mentioned earlier, using pictures minimizes the reading load and allows beginners to exhibit their listening skill without depending on reading ability. Another strategy used with MCQ items includes translating both the stem and the options into test-takers' native language when the test is given to a homogenous group with the same linguistic background.

FIGURE 4.4: Sample Multiple Choice Tasks for Low-Proficiency Language Learners

[Read aloud to test-taker]

1. Draw a circle around the star.

2. Point to the face.

5

We should test only one skill at a time.

In the Real World . . .

A few years ago, a graduate student in one of my doctoral classes submitted a draft of a literature review on Chinese language programs in the United States. (This is Lia.) Reading through the draft, I realized that there were chunks of text in a voice different than my student's. In some cases, she had cited a website; upon checking, I could see the text was copied directly without quotation marks or paraphrasing. In other places, a Google search of a string of words brought up other websites that the student had used. Having taught ESL writing courses for some years, I recognized that this was possibly an issue of not knowing how to integrate sources rather than deliberate plagiarism. During an appointment, I discussed the issue with the student. Despite having taken many years of coursework in English and passing the university's English placement exam, she still had limited knowledge of how reading should be integrated with academic research writing.

As is fairly common in university placement testing, she had been assessed in English with a timed expository essay and a multiple choice reading test (as well as listening and speaking sections of the test) to see if she needed more coursework for success at the university. Results indicated she had the requisite ability in these areas. However, her ability to *integrate* reading and writing in English was clearly limited, yet this skill was not tested. Unfortunately, this conversation between university faculty and students is not unique, and a good deal of literature (Johns & Mayes, 1990; Pennycook, 1996; Plakans & Gebril, 2012, 2013) has addressed the complexities of citation and borrowed text in English for Academic Purposes (EAP). After a series of tutorials with me, her revised paper showed improvement; however, given the high incidence of writing that requires reading; it seems that testing English without considering this ability may be doing a disservice to students.

When we have asked students about integrated reading-writing assessment, they are resoundingly positive about writing tests that include reading, at least in contrast to writing without source material. In a survey we conducted with 145 Arabic-speaking students who had written integrated and independent essays, 75 percent of the students agreed or strongly agreed to the statement, "I like reading about the topic before writing." Their comments illustrate some of the benefits of integrated assessment from a student's point of view:

- "I prefer writing with reading because they make the answer much easier and provide us with information."
- "This is a useful method for getting information. It happens that students sometimes do not have background knowledge on a specific topic about which they are writing and they are required to write reading-based writing. It will help them get information they also read to reflect on the topic."

The myth that skills should be tested separately comes from the perspective that the four skills of reading, writing, listening, and speaking are more clearly defined individually and therefore can be tested more accurately in isolation. There is some truth to this idea and, in certain contexts, testing one skill at a time makes sense. However, research (Fitzgerald & Shanahan, 2000; Sawaki, Quinlan, & Lee, 2013) has shown that some underlying abilities in these skills are shared, and integration may require abilities not captured when testing skills separately (Plakans, 2008, 2009). As the previous story shows, skills are regularly integrated in the "real world" and testing them together may be more authentic.

What the Research Says . . .

Integrated assessment refers to tasks on tests that combine more than one language skill to simulate situations where authentic language is used, such as performance assessments of writing or speaking. An integrated assessment task might require that students listen to a lecture, read a passage, and then write a summary that compares the two texts. Such tasks have recently generated a good deal of interest. The practicality and clarity in such testing, however, have raised concerns.

Can We Really Divide Language into Four Skills?

The decision about whether to test skills together rests in how we think about language: as a compilation of abilities, a set of processes/skills, and/or holistically. The view of testing language as four skills dates back to the 1960s (Cooper, 1965); however, not all skills have been given equal status in language teaching and learning. Over the years, scholars have sometimes considered language skills as competing entities. Schafer (1981) argued that the relationship between speaking and writing has routinely been described in terms of the primacy of one or the other. The audiolingual approach, widely used in the 1970s and '80s, placed the focus on oral skills with written skills taking a backseat (Larsen-Freeman, 2000). In the context of writing instruction, reading and writing have been separated by U.S. university composition programs; Grabe (1986) claims that in the past, experts were recommending ESL reading be taught separately so that it would not be perceived as subordinate to other language skills. Since language testing reflects what is happening in the language classroom, it is no wonder that separation and competition between skills have remained in assessment.

While the view of separate skills has dominated, alternative positions supporting skills integration have also appeared in the literature since the 1960s. Many studies have shown that abilities are shared across the four skills. For example, studies regarding reading-writing connections (Fitzgerald & Shanahan, 2000) have advanced three arguments about their overlap: (1) a rhetorical relationship exists between reading and writing since they are both communicative activities between readers and writers; (2) procedural connections happen when completing academic tasks, which requires skills to be used simultaneously, such as taking notes when reading or reading source material when writing; and (3) the connections between reading and writing occur through shared knowledge and cognitive processes. The third argument has the most research support: while superficially we might see them as separate skills, we find commonalities for each in their sub-skills, such as vocabulary knowledge or text processing. Fitzgerald and Shanahan (2000, p. 41) list the types of knowledge that are used in both reading and writing:

- metaknowledge (pragmatics)
- domain knowledge (prior knowledge, content knowledge)
- knowledge about universal text attributes
- procedural knowledge and skill to negotiate reading and writing.

While their research has focused on L1 readers and writers, other studies investigating integrated tasks with L2 students have also found that the skills share common overarching traits.

Sawaki, Quinlan, and Lee (2013) analyzed 446 TOEFL® integrated writing tests for factors related to reading and listening skills as well as in the writing content. Their findings indicated that the assessment measured three constructs: sentence formation, productive vocabulary, and comprehension. This result contrasts with what we might expect from a separate skills viewpoint, which would identify reading, listening, and writing as the three distinguishable constructs. In sum, research has shown that, in fact, the four skills may not be truly separable but are interdependent through shared sub-skills or higher-order processing (Cumming, 2014). Integrating them in assessment, therefore, may be more natural.

Integrating Skills Is Authentic in EAP

Another research area that supports integrating skills in assessment has examined tasks and authentic language use situations, such as in EAP. Studies have explored the nature of writing tasks and the roles played by other skills in academic writing (Carson, 2001; Elben, 1983; Hale et al., 1996; Horowitz, 1986; Moore & Morton, 1999). For example, Horowitz (1986) reported these integrated skills tasks from a U.S. university context: an annotated bibliography, a summary or reaction to a reading, a connection of theory and data, a report on a specified participatory experience, a case study, a synthesis of multiple sources, and a research project.

Hale et al. (1996) investigated writing tasks from academic courses at eight U.S. universities and found that both graduate and undergraduate courses use a large number of writing tasks that require reading, including summaries, book reviews, and plans/proposals. In Australia, Moore and Morton (1999) collected assignment handouts from two different universities. Their analysis revealed a wide range of writing tasks requiring other skills, including case study reports, research reports, reviews, experimental reports, literature reports, research proposals, and summaries. These studies show strong evidence of skill integration in writing academic English.

Although more studies have focused on writing integration, speaking is also combined with other skills in the academic English context. Ostler (1980) showed that university students, when asked about the most important oral skills needed for their academic success, reported a number of integrated tasks in their classes, including the sequence of taking notes, asking questions about lectures, and participating in discussions about readings. Ferris and Tagg (1996) found integration in oral skills on graded collaborative assignments and when giving informal presentations.

Students May Perform Better on Integrated Skills Assessments

Quotations in the opening section of this chapter (see page 62) present representative positive reactions by the student who had completed an integrated assessment task. If students find assessments meaningful and fair, it can motivate them to do their best. One advantage of integrating skills in language assessment is the background knowledge obtained from source texts. For example, students in a writing context can get information from both reading and listening materials before they compose. Research (Gebril & Plakans, 2013; Leki & Carson, 1997; Plakans & Gebril, 2012, 2013; Weigle, 2004) has shown that students' access to content improves when they complete integrated tasks. Weigle (2004) speaks to this issue:

> Another argument for using a source text as a basis for writing is that it provides a common information source for all test-takers, putting them on a more equal footing in terms of the amount of background knowledge needed to respond to a writing task. Furthermore, a source text can serve to activate the writer's knowledge or schemata around a topic, helping them generate ideas for their writing. (p. 30)

Our research (Plakans & Gebril, 2012) echoed these findings, concluding that test-takers frequently use source texts to get more information about the topic and even generate new ideas. In the same vein, Leki and Carson (1997) concluded that source texts reduce students' workload; they do not have to create as many of their own words and ideas. Likewise, source materials provide very helpful input when testing speaking skills, especially when the topic is relatively new to test-takers or technical in nature. For example, in the case of a reading-to-speak

(RTS) task, Huang and Hung (2010) found "a tremendous preference for the RTS task . . . on the part of the students because its reading element activated and/or furnished background knowledge" (p. 241).

In integrated language assessment, students obtain background knowledge from sources and also use them for language support. In a study we conducted, think-aloud protocols and survey data were collected from writers completing a reading-to-write (RTW) task (Plakans & Gebril, 2012). The analysis of these data found that writers reported that the source materials provided them with language needed for composing their own texts, including technical terminology and the spelling of words. Around 60 percent of the test-takers agreed that they used some words from the source materials while writing, and the same percentage believed that the source materials helped them write better.

The input from source materials, whether written or oral, can also help test-takers organize their ideas. It serves as a model as they structure their arguments. In our study, a writer described how she used the text: "I do prefer reading-based tasks because the ideas and words are present and the task is organized, and I can use the same model. In a writing-only task, I may not find ideas and I do not know how to organize these ideas." In an integrated speaking context, Huang and Hung (2010, p. 241) concluded that the source materials helped to "inspire and guide the oral production task."

Another benefit of source materials is in shaping test-takers' opinions about the topic, especially when developing an argument. In integrated argumentative tasks, source materials often present two opposing views. In our study (Gebril & Plakans, 2009), students were given two texts: one warned about the threat of global warming while the other claimed it was not really a problem. In such tasks, the quality of the argument in the texts and the evidence provided may facilitate the test-taker's choice of an opinion.

What We Can Do . . .

1. Align testing with teaching of integrated skills.

The research refuting the myth about separating skills applies to both testing and teaching. If skills are not really so distinct and occur together in real-life usage, then language teaching probably should teach skills in combination. It is problematic if we test skills in integration but teach them separately, or vice versa.

To elevate integration in language teaching, teachers should instruct students on processes and strategies for successfully completing integrated tasks by using activities that scaffold skill integration. Specifically, teachers should provide students with relevant strategies that focus on how to understand integrated prompts and instructions, approach source materials, synthesize information in written or oral output, and generally fulfill the task requirement. Many current test-preparation courses focus on the aforementioned skills, especially because of the growing interest in integrated assessment and the increasing number of tests that have adopted this approach in test development. For example, in test-preparation courses for the TOEFL® iBT, test instructors spend considerable time training students how to manage source materials and how to use these sources in their writing and speaking. This phenomenon suggests a positive impact on education from these new test tasks. Skill integration instruction should not be limited to test preparation and large-scale testing, however.

2. Write effective integrated tasks for assignments and classroom assessment.

As with any task, careful planning is critical to get meaningful results. Figure 5.1 shows an integrated assessment task that we designed for English learners in the United Arab Emirates to test academic writing (Gebril & Plakans, 2009, 2013). It illustrates some important features to consider when designing an integrated task.

FIGURE 5.1: Sample Reading-Writing Task

Writing Task

Read the question below, and then read the two passages to get more information about the topic. Write an essay on the topic giving your opinion in response to the question. Typically, an effective response will contain a minimum of 300 words. Your writing will be scored based on how well:

- your **ideas** are explained
- the **readings** support your argument
- you **organize** your essay
- you **choose words**
- you **use grammar**
- you **spell** and **punctuate**

Some people believe that global warming is damaging our planet. Others believe that global warming is not a serious problem. Which point of view do you agree with? Why?

Give reasons and support your writing with examples.

IMPORTANT! Please read carefully before working on the task:

- The two passages should help you get some ideas about the topic.
- You may go back to the passages to check information while writing.
- You can borrow ideas and examples from the text. However, you should mention the author's or researcher's name if you do so.
- Also, if you take exactly the same phrases or sentences mentioned in the passage, put them between quotation marks.

Reading 1: Scientists Say Global Warming Is Undeniable

Scientists have confirmed that climate change is being caused by human activity. A number of studies looking at the oceans and melting ice leave no doubt that it is getting warmer, people are to blame, and the weather is going to suffer.

Tim Barnett, who is a famous global warming researcher, indicates that new computer models that look at ocean temperatures instead of the atmosphere show the clearest signal yet that global warming is well underway. Mr. Barnett said that earlier climate models based on air temperatures were weak because most of the evidence for global warming is not in the air.

Other researchers found clear effects on climate and animals. For example, Ruth Curry, who is from an important oceanographic institute, said changes in the water cycle affects the ocean and, ultimately, climate. She said the changes were already causing droughts in the United States, and Greenland's ice cap. Sharon Smith of the University of Miami found melting ice was taking with it plants that are an important base of the food supply for many animals. And the disappearing ice meant that melting ice was changing the animals such as polar bears and seals were losing their homes.

Given all these serious problems caused by global warming and the way humans have abused the earth, governments must act immediately to save our planet. The future of this planet depends on our actions and any delay would result in serious problems.

(Adapted from Reuters, 2005, www.doc.net.au/news/newsitem/200502/51306233.html)

Reading 2: *Myths of Global Warming*

There is no scientific agreement that global warming is a problem or that humans are its cause. Even if current predictions of global warming are correct, much of the environmental policy now proposed is based on wrong theories. First, there is a wrong belief that the earth is warming. While ground-level temperature suggests the earth has warmed between 0.3 and 0.6 degrees since 1850, reliable global satellite data show no evidence of warming during the past 18 years. In addition, scientists do not agree that humans affect global climate because the evidence supporting that theory is weak. Some people also think that the government must act now to stop global warming. However, a 1995 analysis by supporters of global warming theory concluded that the world's governments can wait up to 25 years to take action with no bad effect on the environment. In short, our policymakers need not act immediately. The government has time to gather more data, and industry has time to develop new ways of reducing its influence.

Supporters of the theory of human-caused global warming also argue that it is causing and will continue to cause all environmental problems. Many famous scientists reject these beliefs. Sea levels are rising around the globe, though not equally. In fact, sea levels have risen more than 300 feet over the last 18,000 years. Contrary to the predictions of global warming theorists, the current rate of increase is slower than the average rate over 18,000 years.

(Adapted from an article by Sterling Burnett, a Senior Fellow for the National Center for Policy Analysis, 2001, http://www.ncpa.org/ba/ba230.html)

Task creation in integrated assessment involves two critical steps: (1) the selection of source materials and (2) the development of the task prompt. When selecting source materials for integrated tasks, features of the text can greatly affect the quality of the response. Here are some questions to consider when selecting or writing source texts:

- How many source texts should I give the students? A number of researchers (Gebril, 2009; Weigle, 2004) recommend using two texts for variety and authenticity. Particularly for persuasive writing, the inclusion of two source texts provides convincing arguments for the opposing opinions, as shown in Figure 5.1. We had to choose texts that had arguments that were believable and supported by researchers. Finding a balance can be a challenge with some issues, but should not bias students toward one side by having a text on the opposing side that is quite weak.
- Does the text fit with the purpose of the task and the nature of the prompt? Considering what you want to learn from the results is an important part of text selection. If you hope to assess reading or listening along with writing, for example, you may want source texts that challenge students or include language features studied in class. Also, you might pick different textural genres for an argument (a persuasive text) than you would for summarizing (an informative text).
- Does the level of difficulty of the source text match the proficiency level of the students? Both qualitative and quantitative techniques could be used to check the suitability of a certain text for a specific test population. Readability formulas provide some basic information in determining the difficulty of the text; however, that should not be the only factor. Piloting the source texts is the best assurance of level appropriateness. Based on piloting, we adapted the two readings in the global

warming task (Figure 5.1) by using somewhat less complex sentences and minimizing unnecessarily difficult vocabulary. Other issues, such as familiarity with the selected topic and cultural appropriateness, should be considered by teachers who know the students they are testing.

Task prompts also need careful consideration. If the student/test-taker lacks familiarity with integrated tasks, clear instructions about how to fulfill their requirements are important. The task in Figure 5.1 needed a full page of instructions, including the actual prompt (Which point of view do you agree with? Why?) and specific mention of how to use the readings when writing. Instructions for integrated tasks should include:

- setting the scene for the integrated task through information about the topic, genre, expected length of the response, purpose, and time
- providing guidelines regarding how students should use source materials
- listing the scoring criteria that will be used to assess the response
- guiding students so that they do not plagiarize source material in their responses.

3. Pay careful attention to integration in scoring.

Since integrated tasks are usually performance assessments, the guidelines for scoring and rubric development described in Myth 3 are relevant. When figuring out the criteria for scoring integrated tasks, be sure to focus on aspects of integration, not just language features. Aspects of source use might include the accuracy of ideas taken from the sources or the quality of source integration. Essentially, a scoring rubric that describes the expected performance at different levels must attend to both language and content features. Figure 5.2 shows a scoring rubric for integrated tasks that we developed based on our research and experience with these tasks. The sections of this rubric on source use, development of ideas, and authorial voice all deal with issues related to integration; the criteria for organization and language use are typical rating in writing performance assessment.

Rating or scoring integrated assessments may require some reflection and practice for teachers who are accustomed to assessing single-skill tasks. A good strategy is to try doing the task yourself; think about what is important in the source material, how to use it in your response, and how your performance reflects your ability to synthesize. Practice or collaborate with colleagues to evaluate unique aspects of integrated tasks and reflect on how to judge the quality of discourse synthesis. When working with colleagues on scoring or developing rubrics, it can be useful to look at problematic essays, such as those with ideas copied directly from sources or that misconstrue ideas from the sources. Because of such issues, teachers need to consider scoring carefully: How will you give students feedback on problems and ways they can improve? Integrating source material into writing or speaking is a challenging and multifaceted process that trips up native speakers as well; being able to diagnose where students are struggling is critical for teaching these skills. A good scoring rubric can help to pinpoint which aspects of source use need development.

FIGURE 5.2: An Analytic Rubric for Rating an Integrated Task (Rating scale from 1–5)

Source Use

5—The writing shows high integration quality and accuracy of source text content. Sources were effectively used to address the issues.

4—Source use is relevant and accurate, and generally effective in addressing the issues under discussion.

3—Adequate source use, but not well integrated in the writing. Sometimes source details are misrepresented.

2—Very few instances of source use with inadequate citation and serious problems with the accuracy of source information.

1—No source use or very problematic textual borrowing, either through verbatim use without giving credit to authors or complete misrepresentation of source information.

Comments:

Organization

5—The essay has a clear, logical and effective organizational plan, sophisticated use of cohesive devices, and a solid introduction and conclusion.

4—The essay generally has an adequate organizational plan, making good use of cohesive devices, with a clear introduction and conclusion.

3—The organizational plan is not clear enough, but there is an introduction and a conclusion, and cohesive devices are sometimes used.

2—The organizational plan is weak, few cohesive devices are used, and the argument is not easily followed.

1—No organizational plan is evident and the argument is difficult to follow.

Comments:

Development of ideas

5—Full development of ideas using different types of details provided by the student and support from the source texts.

4—Development is adequate. Details provided by the writer or adapted from the source texts are generally used to support the argument.

3—Development is emerging, and few details that support the argument are provided by the student or adapted from the source texts.

2—Little development in the essay, with hardly any details to support the argument.

1—No development of the topic; the argument is not supported with any details.

Comments:

Language Use

5— Few language errors. The essay includes a variety of sophisticated structures and language accurately presents source and student's ideas.

4— Some language errors that do not result in misrepresentation of source or student's ideas. Varied vocabulary and structures, but redundancy is sometimes an issue.

3— Language errors do not usually interfere with understanding meaning, but may misrepresent the source or student's ideas. Limited variety and common redundancy of structures and vocabulary.

2— Frequent language errors interfere with understanding the essay and misrepresent source ideas, with basic vocabulary and redundant structures.

1— Serious language errors impede understanding, with limited vocabulary and awkward structures.

Comments:

Authorial Voice

5— The essay includes a strong presence of the student with clear personal views that can be easily differentiated from those presented in the source.

4— The essay generally shows the student's identity, and personal views are separated from the source details.

3— The student's identity is sometimes absent, and it is usually hard to distinguish personal views from source views.

2— The essay is mainly a mere reflection of the source views and rarely presents personal views.

1— There is no sense of individuality in the essay, which completely mirrors the source orientation.

Comments:

MYTH 6

A test's validity can be determined by looking at it.

In the Real World . . .

An IEP in which I once worked had a reading placement test consisting of reading passages that included fill-in-the-blank items within the sentences. (This is Lia.) Students had to select the best word from multiple choice options to fit in the blank to complete each sentence. The test was used to place students in appropriate levels of the program's reading courses, which developed skills such as comprehension, fluency, inferencing, and vocabulary knowledge. However, teachers and administrators had little faith in the test scores because we believed they actually measured grammatical knowledge. We wondered if the placement information shouldn't be used for grammar courses rather than reading. The challenges in this situation were related, in part, to validity, which is tied to the **purpose** of the test and the **interpretation** of scores.

The word *validity* is used frequently to refer to the quality of a test, but what does it actually mean? Test publishers sometimes advertise their tests as "valid and reliable." A teacher might intuitively think that a test is not valid when students' scores are very different from their other classwork. What is clear about validity is that it can make or break an assessment. However, understanding how to judge whether the assessment is valid can be much less obvious.

For example, imagine a fill-in-the blank test with these items:

> Write the correct form of the verb in each blank.
> 1. My sister _____ as a hobby.
>   (dance)
> 2. Last week, she _____ for four hours.
>   (dance)

Many language teachers would insist that this kind of a test is not valid because it does not require students to create or produce language. However, it might be considered valid for the *purpose* of testing whether students have understood the difference between simple verb tenses in third-person singular form. In contrast, if it were used to test students' writing ability, its validity would definitely be in question. Validity is not just the quality of a test on the surface, but rather how it is used and for what purpose.

Validity is also related to how we interpret scores from a test. Returning to the fill-in-the-blank example, imagine that students were not given the base word *dance* to insert but only instructed to choose a verb and fill in the blank. How would this affect our interpretation of the score? Would it provide information about both grammar and vocabulary? If one student used the same verb root for all the items, such as *walk*, and another student selected different words for each item, such as *plays guitar* and then *juggled*, does this information help distinguish these two students? Does it mean that one student has more sophisticated vocabulary than the other? What if students used incorrect verb forms for some of the items and unsuitable words for others? Does a low score on the test then indicate that a student does not know verb tenses or that he or she has a limited vocabulary? These various scenarios could lead to complications in interpreting the test score, which gets to the heart of validity in language assessment.

The story about the reading placement test (In the Real World section) had a happy ending. After years of struggling to interpret the scores, the IEP decided to develop its own test in-house. It was based on second language reading theory and took into account the curriculum across the reading course levels when building the test specifications. Teams of teachers developed new reading passages and test questions, which they piloted in their classes. Following this process, a new test was created for reading placement that the teachers trusted because it reflected the students' reading abilities and fit precisely the program's purpose for the test.

What the Research Says . . .

The term *validity* seems to have different meanings depending on who is defining it:

> For many test users, validity is seen as an essential quality of a language test because to them, "a valid test" means "a good test." Accordingly, test users frequently explain their search for a new test or their choice of a test by citing their desire for a test that "has been validated." In using the passive voice . . . users reveal their assumption that validity is a quality of a test that is bestowed by testing experts to make a test measure what it is supposed to. This conception of validity, which requires test users to take little or no responsibility for validity, is at odds with the majority opinion of specialists in educational measurement. (Chapelle, 2012, p. 21)

Because of the complexity of validity as a concept, it can be difficult to determine a test's validity in absolute terms or for every possible context. However, this does not make it any less important. Evidence supporting a test's validity gives confidence to teachers, administrators, and other test users when they use a test for certain purposes with specific students. Validity is an important link in fair and ethical testing.

Evolving Definitions of Validity

The traditional view is that a valid test "measures what it is supposed to measure." While the essence of this definition still holds true, to evaluate a test for validity is much more complex. For some time, test validity was determined by selecting and collecting information on five forms of validity, also called the "toolkit" approach (Chapelle, 1999; Norris, 2008):

- **Construct validity:** The indication that a strong alignment exists between a particular test and the theoretical model of what is being tested. Generally, in language tests, the *construct* is the underlying ability to use language.
- **Content validity:** Evidence that a strong relationship exists between the content that is in the test and the content of the domain for language use. It can also be the connection between test content and course content, sometimes referred to as curriculum validity.
- **Criterion validity:** Evidence that a positive correlation exists between a test score and some other measure that captures the same ability. For example, comparing a student's score on a newly developed reading test with a score on a reading test that has already established credibility can provide the new test with validity evidence.
- **Predictive validity:** As a type of criterion validity, a score is examined in relation to the future performance of the test-taker, such as the correlation between a student's score on the placement test for admittance to a particular course and that student's final grade after completing that course.
- **Face validity:** The intuitive sense that a test looks like it is testing the desired ability or content. Although somewhat superficial, it is a powerful kind of validity,

particularly from a student's point of view, and can affect his or her motivation in performing well on that test.

Validity is often defined in one of these ways, and they each are useful in evaluating an assessment. However, rather than picking and choosing among them, many language testers now view validity as a unified concept found in **construct validity**, an overarching term that subsumes other types of validity evidence. Thus, we may study the different types of validity but understand that they all provide evidence that an assessment is related to an underlying theoretical construct.

For example, we might collect data that support an alignment between test content and the content of a course. These data should substantiate the statement that a learner with a high score on a test has therefore understood the content of the course (content-related validity evidence), which should also be related to a theory of language use. Collected evidence might show a strong positive correlation between performances on daily class assignments and test scores, which would also support the interpretation of a high score as meaning higher ability (criterion-related validity evidence). Both of these types of validity evidence should also support the teacher or the program's philosophy or definition of language ability (construct). With this approach, validity can be viewed along a continuum, not as an all-or-nothing proposition. If strong evidence is collected to support a test score's relation to a chosen construct, then the integrity of the test is strengthened.

Constructs and Construct Validity

In the field of measurement in the 1980s, Cronbach (1988) and Messick (1989) proposed a cohesive view of validity described as construct validity. In language testing construct validity means that the overall judgment of a test's validity should be found in evidence connecting it to a theoretical model of language ability, use, or knowledge. The construct is determined by the **purpose** of an assessment. For example, if a test's purpose is to evaluate students' speaking skills in

Spanish, then a test developer should consider a construct that details Spanish language use, particularly components required for speaking.

Two constructs of language ability can serve to illustrate the relationship between language testing and validity: communicative competence and communicative adequacy. The construct of **communicative competence** has been pervasive in the field since the 1980s (Canale, 1983; Canale & Swain, 1980) (and was discussed in Myth 3). If this construct were used to develop a test of Spanish-speaking ability, then to evaluate its validity we would consider the combination of test tasks, student performances, and scoring rubric in eliciting the components of communicative competence. Tasks that require students to communicate for a specific audience, such as asking a store clerk for help in finding an unusual food item, would likely produce language showing sociolinguistic, linguistic, and discourse competencies. A rating scale that incorporates how students deal with negotiating for meaning and the logical flow of their responses may tap into their strategic and discourse competencies.

Communicative competence has been an important construct for language learning and assessment; however, with changes in the field of second language learning, recent constructs have attempted to feature context and interaction more prominently. One such construct proposed for language assessment is **communicative adequacy**. A group of scholars have investigated this construct in writing assessment (Kuiken, Vedder, & Gilabert, 2010) with the intent to add to research on the Common European Framework of Reference (CEFR) and, specifically, to consider the relationship between communicative adequacy and linguistic complexity in writing assessment. For their study, they defined the construct of communicative adequacy as:

> a task-related, dynamic, and interpersonal construct, focusing both on the communicative task which has to be carried out by the speaker or writer (e.g., writing an email to a friend to suggest a restaurant for dinner) and the way the message is received by the interlocutor (the listener or the reader). (Kuiken, Vedder, & Gilabert, 2010, p. 83)

The researchers point out that, surprisingly, there is no agreement on how to measure communicative adequacy, which may be due to "the absence in the literature of a coherent and clear-cut definition of communicative adequacy as a construct" (p. 82). Their study sets out to make this construct more transparent.

The tasks used to elicit this construct were related to opinions about three non-governmental organizations. After reading descriptions of these organizations, test-takers were asked to explain their choice of the best recipient for a grant as one task and to give an opinion on which organization they would like to see featured in a newspaper article as the other. In the study, a five-point rating scale was used to holistically score **communicative adequacy**. For example, descriptors on the scale for Score Levels 2 and 5 include phrases about argument support, the value of the "contribution," and the benefits of the organization selected:

> **Level 2:** The information that the participant communicates briefly describes the chosen organization, and scarcely describes any of its objectives or any of the people who will benefit from it. The arguments are simple (i.e., single statements not supported by other arguments) and poorly connected to the organization's goals and beneficiaries. The text lacks coherence and is confusing. A weak contribution.

> **Level 5:** The participant contributes complete information about the chosen organization, its objectives, or the people who will benefit from it. The arguments are complex and elaborate (e.g., single or multiple statements supported by other arguments) and clearly connected to the organization's goals and beneficiaries. The text flows smoothly, is coherent, and convincing. A highly successful contribution. (Kuiken, Vedder, & Gilabert, 2010, p. 98)

Thus, using this scale with these tasks should provide information about a student's communicative adequacy. The tasks were designed to elicit interpersonal, task-related, dynamic language, and the scale scores the performances on descriptors related to this construct.

While the tasks and the scale target levels of communicative adequacy, this would not be enough to ensure test validity. Evidence is needed to systematically verify claims made from the scores as well as for the use and purpose of the tests. Students' performances can be studied as data to determine the strength of the claims, uses, and purposes. In their study, Kuiken, Vedder, & Gilabert (2010) explore whether claims can be made about the linguistic complexity of a student's writing based on scores on this assessment. They found that scores on their research tasks had stronger ties to linguistic complexity than to functional qualities, which may have been due to raters' comfort and experience rating for linguistic features rather than communicative adequacy. However, there were significant moderate-to-strong correlations between linguistic complexity and communicative adequacy. This finding indicates that the construct of communicative adequacy and linguistic complexity are connected to each other. Furthermore, they found that the two domains were more balanced at advanced language levels than for lower-proficiency writers, who tended to focus on either linguistic complexity or communicative adequacy. The details of this study illustrate how constructs can be defined and examined for use in language tests, providing not just a foundation on which to design a test, but a means to understand what scores tell us about test-takers.

Constructs such as communicative competence or communicative adequacy can help teachers develop curricula and assessment. With classroom-based assessment, teachers may consider a syllabus or curriculum-based construct, which is relevant to content-related validity. Ideally, a syllabus aligns with the theory of language learning (a construct) used by that language program; however, a syllabus is usually operationalized in terms of learning goals and objectives. In Myth 2, Lia described taking German tests that assessed receptive grammatical knowledge but were not aligned with the German courses she was taking, which followed a communicative language approach. Thus, in the context of the course, the end-of-term test had a problem. A final exam developed with communicative tasks similar to those in the course would have had more validity. It is important to look for such alignment, especially when adopting commercially developed assessments for classroom use. An assessment needs to have synergy with the local classroom context, as represented by the syllabus or curriculum.

Validity Arguments

To explore a test's validity, structured arguments have been proposed for test developers to clarify the process (Kane, 2012; Kane, Crooks, & Cohen, 1999). It may not be a framework easily applied to classroom assessment, but the basic concepts are useful for teachers to understand because this process is important when judging large-scale assessments. In building a validity argument, we determine what claims are made by the test, such as "a student with a high score will be able to write successfully in academic settings." These general claims are then revised to be more specific and to target different parts of a validity argument.

"Bridges" have been used to metaphorically illustrate the areas where evidence is needed to support inferences about assessment; the bridges are inferences that join performances, scores, and real-world use (see Kane, Crooks, & Cohen, 1999, and Chapelle, Enright, & Jamieson, 2008, for detailed explanations of validity arguments and bridges). For example, we make a generalization inference from a score on an oral interview to how a student might perform on other similar speaking test tasks. This inference forms a bridge. We also may wish to make an inference from the test score to how the students would perform in speaking tasks in his or her daily life. This would be another bridge. For each bridge, we need to investigate evidence that supports it as well that which could potentially refute it. Through this process of articulating claims, evidence, and interpretations, we build a validity argument. Chapelle, Enright, and Jamieson (2008) detail the step-by-step process in the TOEFL iBT® validity argument in their book, a good source that clarifies these issues.

Collecting Validity Evidence

This chapter's myth suggests that validity is an identifiable quality of a test, yet we have explained multiple contextual and theoretical factors that make up validity. When developing or adopting a test, we need to collect validity evidence to determine if the assessment is appropriate in our context. Two studies that collect validity evidence will be discussed: The first is by Banerjee and Wall (2006) on exit checklists, and the second is by Plakans on integrated assessment tasks.

Banerjee and Wall (2006) have explored validity and reliability in assessments used to make decisions about students who are exiting a pre–academic English language program and entering full-time academic study. They believed a proficiency test like the International English Language Testing System (IELTS®, a large-scale standardized assessment) might serve as a pre-entry measure, but it did not represent the construct for an EAP program thoroughly enough to use as an exit test. As a solution, their program developed checklists for the purpose of exit assessment and then studied two aspects of validity in terms of the checklists: (1) content relevance and coverage and (2) use and interpretation.

In the first area, the researchers asked language testing experts to review the checklists, and they raised a number of validity issues. For example, some descriptors, such as "can handle heavy reading load" or "participates successfully in class discussions," would be hard for instructors to support with concrete evidence. Problems with consistency across different checklists were also identified in this step.

To evaluate use, three instructors used the checklists as they reflected on past student evaluations. Through interviews with these teachers, Banerjee and Wall (2006) found the strength of the checklists was their efficiency because instructors only needed to check boxes rather than to write detailed evaluations. Teachers found that items on the checklists with clearly available evidence were easiest to judge. When an item was less transparent, they talked with students before making judgments. This study illustrates an approach to adopting a new measure that can increase the level of validity for decision-making in a language program. The observation and interviewing of experts and teachers provides evidence for the valid and reliable use of checklists.

Another example of research on validity that focuses on process is a study examining the underlying ability assessed by integrated writing assessment (like those discussed in Myth 5). The study (Plakans, 2009a) initially looked at theory and research in first language literacy to find a construct of integrated reading and writing that described the underlying processes students use to complete integrated tasks. This construct, which is called **discourse synthesis,** consists of three processes used in reading to write: selecting, organizing, and connecting. They are defined as:

- Organizing occurs when writers think about the overall structure of their writing and the structure of the readings.
- Selecting is when they read and choose ideas from the readings for their writing.
- Connecting includes both linking ideas in their writing and connecting the ideas in the readings with their own. (Plakans, 2009a, p. 568)

To investigate the construct validity of integrated tasks, I asked writers to compose responses to an integrated writing task about globalization (see page 100) while thinking aloud, and then, they were interviewed after completing the task.

Globalization has had a strong impact on the world. One issue of globalization is cultural borrowing or adaptation.

- Read the following passages about this issue.
- Then consider your opinion about the impact of globalization on culture.
- Plan and write an essay supporting your position and using examples.
- Incorporate relevant information from the passages appropriately. Do not copy exact phases; cite the authors.

Your writing will be evaluated on:
a. content
b. organization
c. grammar and vocabulary
d. punctuation and spelling.

Readings: [the task included two passages on globalization and culture, each 200 words in length]

After transcribing the think-alouds and interviews from the testing sessions, data were coded for the three processes: organizing, selecting, and connecting. The results indicated that the higher-scoring writers followed the discourse synthesis process while lower-scoring writers spent more time and attention on basic reading skills such as comprehension and understanding vocabulary. These results indicate that discourse synthesis provided a potential construct for integrated writing tasks on which to collect further validity evidence and to develop assessments.

In sum, validity is a test quality that requires thoughtful, ongoing consideration beyond surface appearances. While the approaches to conducting validation studies evolve and expand, we also have to consider the kind of evidence that will allow us to make the desired claims about scores from our assessments given our specific purposes and particular contexts.

What We Can Do . . .

While some approaches to validity evidence gathering are quite complex, there are basic practices that language teaching professionals can adopt.

1. Ask why you are assessing students and what your view of language is.

When adopting a commercial or standardized test for a language program, the purpose for which the test is designed should correspond to the purpose for which it will be used. For example, proficiency tests may not be best for making language program exit decisions, as Banerjee and Wall (2006) have pointed out. It may be better to develop checklists or portfolios to answer questions and make such decisions. Or perhaps a test for multiple purposes, such as for placement and for diagnostic information, might be chosen; however, one must carefully consider whether dual purposes are feasible and if the information gained from the assessment really fulfills both needs.

The second part of the question, about your "view of language," relates to constructs. Language courses and programs should be based on a definition of what language ability is in terms of use, specific purposes, skills, and so forth. This definition is part of curriculum development and should underlie all practices in the program, including assessment. Even though a construct of language ability may be implied by teaching practices and appear in program documents, articulating it can help elevate the validity of the assessments used in a course or program.

2. Use multiple measures to evaluate students.

Tests are sometimes labeled as high stakes or low stakes, but for students, the stakes may always feel high. Decisions made as a result of assessment should consider multiple sources of information. If only one test score is used to determine placement, exit, or proficiency, the likelihood of error increases. Collecting several measures or considering a test along with other reports on student performance can lead to more confident decision-making.

Using multiple sources has at least two advantages:

1. We gain more evidence about the student's language skills, which creates a more detailed profile. For example, tests are often constrained by time, taken in one sitting on one day, and thus cannot provide evidence for a learner's ability to improve over time. However, a portfolio of work from a full semester or term could fill this gap. Affective responses to tests, such as anxiety or nervousness, can also influence a learner's performance. Having other measures can mitigate this reliability issue that has implications for validity.

2. If the various information sources align well, they can be evidence for the validity of the assessment score interpretations.

3. Critique the tests you are using.

Validity in assessment practices can be improved by systematically considering ways of revising tests to make them better; in other words, believing and acting as if a good test is never "done." Even published language tests evolve as research and revisions are ongoing. Post-test information gathering and reflection are part of the test designing process. Once students have taken a test, a number of approaches can be used to delve into its usefulness:

- Compare the assessment to other information gathered about these students to check on the test. If a lot of variability occurs in a student's performances on different measures, follow up to see if this is due to language development or because of assessment issues. Compare scores among the students to see if there is a range or if they all received nearly the same score on the test. This can tell you if scoring is providing useful information to distinguish between their proficiency.

- Ask students afterward to talk through what they did while they were taking the test. This provides insights into processes that cannot be captured directly by the scores. This kind of feedback can reveal if students were guessing or if they answered incorrectly because they did not understand the instructions. These sorts of testing issues that impede the validity of score interpretation can only be ascertained by getting student feedback.

- Interview teachers, as Banerjee and Wall (2006) did. Teacher insights on program-wide tests, like those for placement or exiting, can clarify how efficient and effective these assessments are, identify issues of validity, and point out areas in need of revision.

Issues of fairness are not a concern in standardized testing.

In the Real World . . .

I always dreamed of completing my PhD studies in the United States. (This is Atta.) I wanted to specialize in language testing, and for that reason I decided on a short list of potential programs at some U.S. universities. I started preparing graduate applications and had to take a language proficiency test, one of the requirements for nonnative English–speaking applicants. Checking on the Internet, I learned the closest testing center for me was in Cairo. At that time, I lived in Sohag, a city in southern Egypt almost 400 kilometers from Cairo. I had to take a seven-hour train ride just to register for the test at the testing center. In addition, it seemed a good opportunity to buy a test-preparation kit while there because these materials were not available in Sohag. Since I had advanced language proficiency, I felt I did not need any test-preparation classes in Cairo and decided to study on my own. However, many of my colleagues whose academic background was in the sciences took these courses. They had to pay not only for the course, but also for their living expenses in Cairo. Some of those who had full-time jobs even took leave from work to have more time for test preparation.

Two days before the exam date, I traveled again to Cairo and stayed in a hotel for the duration of testing. Fortunately, I got scores that were higher than the cut-off scores required by all the graduate programs on my list. However, this was not the case for many of my colleagues who had taken the test with me. In fact, one of them took the test ten times before getting the required score. The cost of the test for this colleague was then equal to one-month's salary. The combination of the cost of the test-preparation courses plus living expenses near the test center meant that many test-takers spent on average almost a year's salary to obtain the required test score.

One of the problems many of us encountered was our unfamiliarity with the format of the test items. I had not taken a single multiple choice test during my undergraduate years in Egypt. Exams at public universities in Egypt at that time primarily used an essay format with an average of only three or four questions that had to be answered in detail. For this reason, preparing for the proficiency test was relatively strange for many examinees. I know that I felt more comfortable working on constructed-response questions than on objective items.

I had many questions about the fairness of proficiency tests at that time: Why did I have to travel twice for seven hours just to take the test that took less than five hours? Why did I have to leave home and stay in a hotel? I envied test-takers who lived close to the testing center in Cairo and did not have to go through this ordeal. They also had access to test-preparation classes in their area. I also wondered about people who couldn't afford to pay for classes or afford the testing fees. And I wondered if those in charge (test administrators, admission officers, test developers) were aware of the costs in time, money, and stress that test-takers were enduring. Since I took that test, some of these inconveniences have improved, and the test is offered in more cities, and test-preparation classes are available in every part of the country.

This chapter is about fairness issues that are typically present in a testing context. A range of issues reflects the complex nature of fairness.

One concerns access. Do all test-takers have equal access to test prepa-ration resources? Are they all familiar with the testing format? These questions relate to **educational** access, but **geographical** access is another issue.

What the Research Says . . .

The Dictionary of Language Testing defines **test fairness** as being:

> concerned with the consequences of testing for individuals, groups or society as a whole. It relates both to the *validity* of a given test as an index of *ability* and to the whole testing process insofar as it reflects or contributes to social equity. (Davies et al., 1999, p. 199)

Such a comprehensive definition encompasses a number of variables at the societal, individual, and test-related levels. Kunnan (2000) sug-gests a framework in language testing that examines fairness from three perspectives—validity, access, and justice:

- **Validity** is at the heart of fairness since unfair practices can affect test scores by including construct-irrelevant variables. Alleviating unfair practices can make the score a better indicator of someone's ability, thereby enhancing score validity.
- **Access** issues are also important for fairness. Resources should be accessible to all examinees to ensure none are disadvantaged because of a lack of resources.
- **Justice** is concerned with testing from the test-taker's point of view. We need to make sure that examinees are treated equally and that no one is favored or disadvantaged because of gender, race, language, or affiliation.

Given the myriad of concerns addressed in fairness, disagreements and debates are not uncommon among stakeholders over what issues to include in this enquiry. Zieky (2006) argues that professionals still do not agree on what constitutes fairness and refers to the contradictory definitions of fairness in the literature. Cole and Zieky (2001) show the discrepancy in the definitions adopted by measurement professionals compared to those espoused by the general public. Assessment specialists typically focus on technical issues when investigating fairness, while the public wants a more serious discussion of specific access issues. The discrepancy between these views has led to many misconceptions about test fairness.

Learning Opportunities and Tests

One reason for misconceptions concerns confusing test fairness with what is called "opportunity to learn," a term coined by Carroll in the 1960s and used to refer to whether students have had sufficient access to education (Tate, 2001). Research (Abedi & Herman, 2010) shows that a number of variables affect opportunities to learn, such as parents' education, poverty, inequitable schooling conditions, quality of teachers, and availability of extracurricular activities. Undoubtedly, an opportunity to learn (or a lack thereof) affects students' test scores. As Camili (2006) argues, what "examinees know in any given situation is a mixture of educational and personal experiences that is strongly affected by access and opportunity to learn" (p. 251).

Abedi and Herman (2010) found a strong relationship between opportunity to learn and test performance, suggesting that limited opportunity to learn might play a role in depressed test scores of some examinees. Zieky (2006) also speaks about the intersection between opportunity to learn and fairness:

The definition of fairness as equality of scores across groups is clear, popular, and wrong. It is wrong because it overlooks the possibility that there may be valid (real and relevant) differences between the groups in what the test is appropriately measuring.

To demonstrate that differences alone are not proof of bias, consider yardsticks. Even though men and women have different average heights, yardsticks are not necessarily biased. (p. 361)

This quotation cautions us about how to interpret group differences in an assessment context. Unfairness cannot be established unless there is clear evidence that some construct-irrelevant variables are at play. For example, differences in scores between test-takers who come from diverse socioeconomic strata do not necessarily mean that the test is biased. Affluent students may be exposed to much richer educational experiences and raised in families where parents have university degrees. These students usually have had access to better learning opportunities outside of school. All these factors can affect their performance in school and consequently their test performance. In such cases, a test that measures learning is not unfair because learning is part of the construct measured, and the test is identifying this difference in learning opportunities. The test alone cannot remedy the inequality existing in society because of variable learning opportunities, which must be done by other means.

Reviewing Tests for Fairness

Large-scale assessment programs usually take serious measures to ensure that their tests are fair and accessible to test-takers. Zieky (2006) refers to the increasing attention paid to fairness issues in professionally developed exams, including citing fairness reviews, which is one of the most common procedures used. Ravitch (2003) defines a fairness review as "an elaborate, well-established protocol of beneficent censorship, quietly endorsed and broadly implemented by textbook publishers, testing agencies, professional associations, states, and the federal government" (p. 3). Educational Testing Service (ETS) long ago established committees of outside testing experts who review the content of its various tests using clear guidelines described in the *ETS Guidelines for Fairness Review of Assessments* (ETS, 2009). Items that raise fairness issues are revised or removed from tests as an attempt to ensure that test-takers are treated equitably.

From the perspective of validity, test fairness is usually discussed within the context of how scores are affected by variables unrelated to the construct (they are **construct irrelevant**). Test developers are interested in investigating whether issues such as bias, topical knowledge, or culture-specific materials have had an impact on test scores. Bias generally occurs when a specific group is disadvantaged by certain test content. Groups may include test-takers from a specific ethnic or linguistic background (Abbott, 2007; Kim & Jang, 2009) or they may be classified based on other variables, such as gender (Pae & Park, 2006; Takala & Kaftandjieva, 2000). Elder (2013) referred to other bias sources, including instructional experience and background knowledge as well as interaction between raters and specific groups.

When investigating bias in test items, test developers usually consider these questions:

1. *Does the test content have an equal representation of different ethnic and gender groups?*
   - Do images include people from different ethnic groups?
   - Are female and male names represented equally?
   - In terms of job titles and social roles, are different groups equally represented?

2. *Is there any language-related bias?*
   - Is there any offensive language on the test?
   - Is there any sexist language on the test?
   - Is there any technical vocabulary that may not be familiar to some test-takers?

3. *Is there any content-related bias?*
   - Does the test content perpetuate any stereotypes about a specific segment of the test population?
   - Does the test content include any potentially offensive materials targeting a specific segment of the test population?

- Does the test include technical knowledge that favors a specific segment of the test population?
- Does the test include cultural knowledge that favors a specific segment of the test population?

4. *Is there any bias related to item format?*
    - Are there any clues in test items that provide unintended hints to a specific segment of the test population?
    - Are the instructions understood similarly by different groups?
    - Is there a specific item format that favors a segment of the test population?

Research on bias has employed different types of qualitative and quantitative techniques. Differential item functioning (DIF) is a common quantitative methodology used to detect bias in test items. DIF is a statistical procedure to detect differences between groups whose members have the same ability. Item response theory (IRT) is a technique used to investigate DIF in large-scale testing. (Since the calculation of DIF is beyond the scope of this book, readers may want to consult Camili [2006] for a detailed description of this technique.)

In a DIF analysis with two groups of test-takers (for example, men and women) who have the same proficiency level, both groups are expected to perform similarly on a language test. If their performance differs markedly on a particular test item, however, bias may exist in this item because of gender, thus unfairly favoring one group of test-takers over another. Research on bias is used to inform test developers about potential problems so that test items can be revised accordingly. Items found to have bias should undergo content analysis and modification. Still, caution is warranted when interpreting these results because DIF is not sufficient for investigating fairness. Qualitative techniques, especially logical analysis of test items by content experts, are also important in ensuring bias-free assessments.

Fairness in the Classroom

For teachers, fairness is addressed by adhering to the validity guidelines as discussed in Myth 6—in particular, checking assessments for connection to purpose, course content, and syllabus—and a construct of language ability. Research has also explored the issue of fairness in our use of assessments (Shohamy, 2000) and in our classroom practices (Cheng & Wang, 2007).

Several areas of fairness have been identified in students' expectations. Rodabaugh (1996) categorized college students' perceptions of fairness as interactional, procedural, and outcomes-based. Interactional fairness is related to teacher-student relations, such as impartiality, concern for students, respect, and integrity—behavior highly valued by students. The latter two categories, procedural and outcomes fairness, directly involve testing and assessment in classes and deserve a closer look.

Procedural fairness involves issues with course workload, tests, feedback, and student input. In terms of tests, Rodabaugh (1996) points out that fair practice entails returning students' tests promptly with discussion of scoring and items or tasks that many students missed. Giving students feedback on where they did well and where they need to improve also promotes procedural fairness. Some scholars (Whitley et al., 2000) have pointed out that students consider the alignment between course content and test content as a fairness issue. Also related to test quality, but perceived as fairness, is clarity of the test questions and tasks. Test difficulty should also be considered and monitored carefully based on the students in a class; tests should not be designed to fail or weed out students and teachers should not give students a test designed for higher-proficiency learners just to push them. Last, according to Rodabaugh (1996), teachers should allow students to give feedback or ask questions about tests or assignments, either to clarify understanding or to explain questions they found unreasonable.

Outcomes fairness lies in assigning students' final grades or reporting at the end of a learning sequence. Students expect the grade that they feel they deserve and when this does not occur, it may be considered unfair by students. This match or mismatch can be problematic if students' expectations are unrealistic, which should further encourage teachers to be transparent about assessment procedures from the beginning of a course. To improve outcomes fairness, teachers should be vigilant in reviewing and revising assessments that lead to course grades to ensure that they readily reflect students' abilities toward course goals and objectives. Having multiple measures, as discussed with validity, also serves this purpose, because multiple measures can provide a more robust picture of a student's ability both for the student and for grading. Being clear about grading procedures and not changing policies mid-course are other ways to establish and maintain outcomes fairness. These fairness practices are important for trust between students and teachers; in many cases, administrators should establish these as expected practices in schools or programs to ensure consistency and fairness (Whitley et al., 2000). Having programmatic fairness requirements for all classes will also provide new teachers with guidelines to follow. This practice will encourage fair practice and give all teachers and students support when disagreements arise.

Cheng and Wang (2007) interviewed university English teachers in Hong Kong, China, and Canada about assessment practices that can be related to procedural and outcomes fairness, namely grading, feedback, and reporting of grades to students. Most teachers reported that they developed their own scoring criteria to grade assessments, but they were divided in terms of sharing this with students. Most of the teachers in Canada and Hong Kong had different strategies for sharing their scoring criteria with students, such as handouts, class discussion, demonstrations, or through examples. Less than half of the teachers from China reported informing students of the scoring criteria. Most teachers interviewed said that they provided students with written feedback and reported giving students scores or marks on assessments within one or two weeks. Cheng and Wang asked teachers about the follow-up activities conducted after assessments, with teachers in all three contexts focusing on students' errors. Teachers described using individual tutorials as well as whole class discussions to follow up after tests.

Another area of the Cheng and Wang (2007) study that delved into fairness, from students' perspectives, was how teachers reported final grades. They found that percentages were used and oftentimes converted into a letter grade. Points out of 100 were utilized as well as simply a pass or fail decision. This question was followed by the issue of whether students could appeal a grade; the Canadian teachers were split on this issue, while the Hong Kong teachers largely agreed that there was a formal appeal policy, and the majority of Chinese teachers felt there was not. Cheng and Wang mention in their discussion that these teachers seemed to follow fair practice. What makes this study interesting is that it highlights the different aspects of language teaching that fall into the domain of procedural and outcomes fairness, which are often not discussed in language assessment training.

Fairness, Access, and Society

Another major issue of interest in fairness research is the concept of access. Kunnan (2000) provides a taxonomy of access issues that are usually addressed when investigating test fairness. He argues that access investigation should start early in the test development process to make sure that the infrastructure needed for equitable access is in place. Many access issues raised in this section could be investigated by surveying test-takers about the availability of these resources. In addition, research projects looking into access-related technical aspects should make use of quantitative techniques, such as DIF.

Kunnan's taxonomy looks into whether a test is accessible to test-takers by addressing various types of access: "financial, geographical, personal, and educational access and familiarity of test conditions and equipment" (p. 4). For example, financial access would be whether test-takers can afford the test fees. The surge in the fees of international proficiency tests used to make a wide range of admission decisions in academic contexts may impede lower-income test-takers from pursuing an academic degree simply because they did not have the necessary financial resources to take the test. Geographical access focuses on the availability of testing centers so that test-takers do not have to travel long distances to take a test. Personal access addresses the availability of accommodations for test-takers with special needs. For example, visually challenged students will need alternative methods of assessment to assure that they are not disadvantaged by the standard test format. Another area concerns educational access and learning opportunities for students and, finally, the familiarity of test-takers with the testing format (essay, short answer, or multiple choice) and medium (paper or computer). For example, when a computer-based version TOEFL®(CBT) was introduced, a major concern was the computer literacy required of everyone taking this test. Limited experience in using a computer, which was construct-irrelevant, might have easily confounded test scores.

Thinking about access in more depth, an article about schools, textbooks, and standardized tests provides a vivid illustration of fairness problems. A professor of data-journalism traced issues of access in a major urban school district in the United States with a high rate of poverty (Broussard, 2014). She found that knowledge being assessed on state-required standardized exams was linked to the content or problem-solving strategies found in specific textbooks, rather than to general knowledge. She determined that the publishers of certain tests were also the publishers of textbooks that were purchased by schools as curriculum sets, including workbooks, worksheets, etc. In this case, if the textbooks were good representations of what should be learned, then the test-to-textbook alignment might not be a grave issue; what Broussard discovered, however, was that schools and students did not have equal access to these textbooks. Problems with the record-keeping along with limited budgets resulted in some schools with no textbooks, limited copies or outdated textooks, or textbooks not containing the information and logic included in the standardized tests. One parent even reported that the schools were so worried about the scarcity of books that her child was not allowed to bring textbooks home for fear they would get lost.

This article highlights an access problem in assessment that has major consequences for students, teachers, parents, and administrators in the school district. Broussard (2014) proposes to stop the standardized testing while the schools find solutions to remedy the inequality of access in the system. In addition to the issue with access, the author mentioned the growing trend of using such test scores to evaluate teacher quality. Interpreting these scores as reflective of teaching is highly problematic, both because of textbook problems and, as discussed in Myth 6 (validity), the tests were not designed for this purpose. Too many factors, some construct-irrelevant, appear to be affecting the tests, making score interpretation difficult and potentially unfair.

While some access issues are addressed within assessment programs, others are beyond their scope and should be treated from the angle of social justice. Even though test developers can follow certain procedures to alleviate bias, society as a whole needs to take serious actions to minimize inequity. Fairness should be considered as a continuum, not as all-or-nothing proposition. Adopting a social justice framework and considering the complex nature of related issues helps to understand fairness better.

The concept of justice looks into fairness in society at large. Although language educators may feel they cannot control many of these variables, a general understanding of the relevant aspects and sensitivity to societal equity and the consequences of tests is part of assessment literacy. According to Stobart (2005), fairness should not be isolated from educational opportunities, quality of schooling, or from the curriculum on which the assessment is based. This view of fairness is more inclusive and requires policymakers, educational administrators, and other stakeholders in the community to make assessment their concern. These issues must be viewed from a wider perspective to address inequities in educational opportunities and social bias in the society at large. Books by Shohamy (2001) and McNamara and Roever (2006) provide detailed discussions of issues of social justice in language assessment.

Final Comments on Fairness

In reviewing the literature on fairness, it is not our intention to deny the existence of bias in education in general and assessment in particular, nor do we agree that tests can be relied upon to instill fairness. Fairness is a problem to address in assessment programs and at the societal level as well. At the micro level, as language educators, professional guidelines and practices should guide us in developing and using tests fairly. Gipps (1999) calls for transparency and openness when discussing fairness issues:

> The best defense against inequitable assessment is openness. Openness about design, constructs, and scoring will bring out into the open the values and biases of the test design process, offer an opportunity for debate about cultural and social influences, and open up the relationship between the assessor and the learner. (p. 385)

What We Can Do . . .

While many of the fairness issues discussed concern large-scale assessment, fairness is also a concern for language teachers. In addition to these four guidelines, suggestions for practice (What We Can Do) presented in other chapters of this book, particularly in Myths 6 and 8, feed into fairness.

1. Be transparent in assessment procedures.

As the Gipps quotation on this page states, openness is a critical piece of fairness. This applies to classroom teachers as much as it does to testing companies. Teachers have to develop assessment criteria that are clear, realistic, and reflective of the content and skills covered in class. Once assessment criteria are determined, students should receive adequate information about the test content and the scoring criteria to be used to judge their performance. According to Shepard (2000), informing students about assessment criteria not only satisfies a fairness requirement but also helps them "improve learning and develop metacognitive knowledge for monitoring [their] own efforts" (p. 60). For example, in the context of a writing assessment, a scoring rubric with adequate information about the various writing features to be considered and the relative weight of each feature should be shared with the students. Any changes in rubric descriptors or weight of different features should be communicated well before testing occurs so students have enough time to prepare. Implementing approaches such as Assessment for Learning, which includes students in the testing process, would help in promoting the transparency in classroom assessment.

Tests are one area of classroom assessment, but other factors are often considered in evaluative grading and require transparency. For example, including a participation grade to promote student involvement is a common feature on syllabi. Another example common in classes with a range of language abilities is a grade that reflects improvement. While there is value in promoting both of these aspects of learning, the way these grades are handled can be confusing and opaque to students. Unless a teacher defines participation clearly and keeps track of how students participate, such grades could be rather subjective and open to debate. Making grading practices transparent is critical for fairness from a student's perspective.

2. Make tests accessible.

Every student needs equal access to resources for test preparation and information on how tests will be administered. The starting point in making assessments accessible is providing equal opportunities for learning. Students should have the chance to adequately learn the content on which the test is based as well as have access to all test-preparation materials. The example given (see page 114) that described schools lacking textbooks that contain valuable content for succeeding on tests is testament to a system failing to be fair. Broussard (2014) described the teachers in this school district as having an "underground economy" for acquiring textbooks. They negotiated for them with schools that were closing, ran fundraising campaigns to buy materials, and estimated spending $30–1,000 of their own money to buy supplies needed in their classrooms. Increasing accessibility for students should not be the burden of teacher alone. All stakeholders need to be active in ensuring that all students have equal access to learning opportunities.

Providing access for students with special needs is also important to ensure test fairness. Accommodations needed by physically challenged test-takers should be provided. Issues of financial and geographical access are difficult to manage by teachers. However, because information technology has made access to materials much easier, assessment dynamics are continually improving. With increasing levels of computer literacy among students, many language programs can now offer tests online, which improves access for some special needs.

3. Attend to fairness in classroom practices.

Combined with transparency and access, teachers should carefully consider how assessment is implemented for grading and decision-making. These practices can improve procedural and outcomes fairness in the eyes of students:

- Return assessments promptly.
- Go over assessments with students. Discuss commonly missed items, share class patterns of strengths and weaknesses, and explain grading schemes and scoring rubrics.
- Give feedback that students can understand and use to improve scores.
- Review tests for content validity, construct validity, and level of difficulty.

- Be conscious of external reliability issues; for example, provide a quiet, distraction-free environment for testing to minimize students' anxiety as much as possible.
- Allow students to voice their concerns about assessments.
- Be clear about grading policies.
- Provide students with regular feedback on their learning
- Include multiple measures in grading and assessment used in decision-making.

4. Consider diversity in assessments.

Recognizing diverse student populations and being sensitive to their unique needs can help teachers avoid many common fairness problems. Knowing your students not only helps in avoiding fairness pitfalls but also guides assessment practices in schools. The *ETS Fairness Guidelines* (ETS, 2009) list a number of variables that should be attended to during test development. When developing or selecting classroom tests, teachers should consider these variables: ethnicity, disability, gender, native language, religion, age, socioeconomic status, and national or regional origin. When writing classroom tests, each item should be checked to ensure that it does not favor a specific group over others.

The content selected for a test can be a source of construct-irrelevant difficulty. For example, specialized knowledge embedded in language tests can be a major problem if a test is administered to a diverse group of students with different academic backgrounds. Often technical vocabulary is a source of difficulty for those unfamiliar with a specific field. If medical terminology is included in the reading passages of a language test, for example, students from non–health related fields may be disadvantaged and, consequently, their performance on the test could be negatively affected. In such cases, a construct-irrelevant variable is affecting score validity because the results do not accurately reflect the language ability measured on the reading test; lack of background knowledge is confounding the students' performance.

Offensive or taboo topics should also be avoided when writing test content. Such content could disturb students from specific cultures, ethnicities, regions, religions, or genders. If dating practices or drinking alcohol are not allowed in certain cultures, such topics should be avoided when writing tests for students from those cultures. Stereotyping is also a source of offensive content perpetuating negative images of a specific group. According to the Fairness in Testing Manual of the Data Recognition Corporation (2003, p. 3), stereotyping in test content can include "physical characteristics, intellectual characteristics, emotions, careers, activities, and domestic or social roles."

Topics that are culturally loaded or require cultural knowledge should also be avoided. Ravitch (2003) lists a number of cultural topics that U.S. fairness review committees usually avoid: birthday celebrations, Christmas, Halloween, spiders, supernatural powers, junk food, and social dancing. Another culturally loaded example of content is humor, since it could be misunderstood by various groups of students; in fact, they might be offended. Language about human body parts is a third example of content that may embed cultural knowledge and could be misinterpreted. For example, if tests include images with hand gestures, one has to determine if the signals will be understood similarly by all test-takers.

Teachers should not be involved in preparing students for tests.

In the Real World . . .

When I was a high school student (this is Atta), I had to take the Egyptian General Secondary School Certificate Exam, which is called the *thanaweya amma* test. This is used as an exit test from high school and also for university entrance purposes—actually the only indicator used by Egyptian universities for making admission decisions. I heard all kinds of stories from older students about their experience with the test and the things they had done to prepare for it. Listening to their advice, I began preparing for the *thanaweya amma* test almost a year before its scheduled date. Two months before the beginning of the academic year in September, I made reservations for private tutoring by a teacher recommended by my older friends.

This was and still is the most common way of preparing for this test in Egypt: hiring a teacher to spend an hour or two every week with students outside of regular school hours. Language practice and communicative activities were not included in these sessions at all. The relatively narrow scope of private tutoring mainly revolved around teaching-to-the-test activities; the tutor focused on how to answer the various question types that typically appear on the test. During school hours, teachers attempted to cover content areas and skills included in the textbooks, but there was huge pressure from students (and sometimes their families) just to use class time to focus primarily on the skills included on the *thanaweya amma* test.

Since the test does not include any speaking or listening items, these skills tended to be given less attention or completely ignored, especially near the end of the year when pressure mounted and students demanded more test-related activities. At my school right before the exam, review activities in the examination subjects overshadowed the non-examination subjects, such as music and physical education, which were downplayed.

Newspapers even used to publish daily reviews and likely test items. I still remember a week or two before the exam going to a kiosk early every morning to buy a newspaper containing a section on test-preparation tips. After the test, newspapers also comprehensively covered the performance of students on every single subject and their reactions toward the test items. Surprisingly, most of this testing frenzy is still common today in Egypt.

My experience is a good example of how the test-preparation industry thrives in high-stakes assessment contexts. Egyptian society's preoccupation with this test is due to the crucial decisions based on its results and, accordingly, the dominating competitive atmosphere that exists. Such pressure is quite common in many countries and clearly contributes to negative myths about test preparation and teaching to the test. However, this attitude oversimplifies how teaching and testing interact.

What the Research Says . . .

The relationship between teaching and testing is complex and dynamic. This connection is affected by the changing role of assessment in schools and the way policymakers use tests either to make decisions about the future of students or to monitor instructional practices. Assessment serves as a gatekeeper for selection, diagnosis, placement, and exit decisions. As far as monitoring instructional practices, assessment also currently attempts to make schools accountable in many countries. Student learning is frequently assessed by externally mandated standardized tests. Their performance on these exams determines the types of rewards or sanctions each school receives. Such policies increase pressure on teachers to prepare their students to score well on these exams and improve their test scores. Consequently, when test preparation moves away from learning-oriented activities, developing language proficiency of students is no longer a priority in schools. This can make test preparation "bad practice."

We would argue, however, that test preparation has the potential to be good if it leads to more meaningful test scores and is genuinely connected to learning. A famous scholar in the field of educational measurement, Messick (1996), once stated, "There should be little, if any, difference between activities involved in learning the language and activities involved in preparing for the test" (pp. 241–242).

Important Terms Related to Test Preparation

A number of terms have been used in the educational assessment literature to refer to the dynamic relationship between assessment and instruction: **washback, test impact, curriculum alignment,** and **teaching to the test,** to mention a few. Given the complex nature of these concepts, it is important to clarify their meanings.

Washback, sometimes called **backwash,** refers to a particular test's effects (whether negative or positive) on teaching and learning (Cheng, Watanabe, & Curtis, 2004; Wall, 1997). The Egyptian *thanaweya amma* test is a good example of negative washback. Since speaking and listening are not tested, these skills are given short shrift or entirely ignored by students and teachers. The results are poor oral skills among students in Egyptian schools. Washback can also be positive, especially when tests improve instructional practices. For instance, the TOEFL® iBT test, which includes integrated writing assessment, has had positive effects on the teaching of academic writing. Since integrated writing involves the use of reading with writing, students and teachers alike have started to pay more attention to skills such as selecting important ideas from reading to use in writing and paraphrasing without plagiarizing in addition to basic writing development (Gebril, 2009; Plakans & Gebril, 2013).

Another related term, **test impact**, has a wider scope than washback and includes the effects of tests both inside the classroom and outside in society at large. An example from the *thanaweya amma* context is the emotional and financial strain Egyptian families endure while their teenagers prepare and take that test. Statistics from the Egyptian Central Agency for Public Mobilization and Statistics (CAPMAS) show that 42 percent of Egyptian household spending is allotted to pay for private tutoring (CAPMAS, 2013). As an example, this quotation comes from an article that appeared in *Al-Ahram Weekly* in May 2012, which is one of the oldest and most prestigious newspapers in Egypt:

> Money wise or because of the emotional strain, the *thanaweya amma* or General Certificate for Secondary Education, is known for being a severe burden on families. Customary private tutoring swallows up family incomes while the acceptance in universities will depend on students' grades in this fateful last year of high school. . . . Teachers consider the private lessons of *thanaweya amma* one of the most rewarding businesses in the country, but parents say they are the most financially challenging. Private tutoring has become a prerequisite for passing the year. The impact of *thanaweya amma* exams falls directly on the entire household. For students and parents, a state of emergency is always announced at the homes of all *thanaweya amma* students, sometimes a year in advance.

Months before the school year starts, private lesson reservations are made to guarantee that the student will find a place with the preferred private teacher. . . . Egypt's education system is in dire need of an overhaul, according to Mostafa Bakri (Member of Parliament). He said instead of wasting LE 3 billion (Egyptian pounds) on private lessons, less than half of this amount could be used in improving the education system, schools, curriculums and teachers. (Leila, 2012)

Teaching to the test can result in students who are "test wise," but who miss important educational opportunities. **Test wiseness,** or **test-besting skills,** refers to skills that can help examinees answer specific questions without having much real knowledge. Teaching these skills is not recommended since they can lead to inflated conclusions about examinees' abilities and cause test score pollution. **Score pollution** is a product of being test wise. The score includes inaccuracies that are not related to the knowledge or construct this assessment tool is intended to test, such as the ability to match words in multiple choice questions to words in a reading passage, rather than comprehending the passage.

In general educational assessment circles, the term **curriculum alignment** refers to the process of relating tests to content standards that document the skills and topics covered in curricula. For example, TESOL International publishes standards for ESL teaching in pre-kindergarten though secondary grades (PreK–12). Standard 1 reads, "English language learners communicate for social, intercultural, and instructional purposes within the school settings" (TESOL, 2006). For curricular alignment, a program would consider how to integrate assessments in coursework to evaluate if ELLs were able to meet this standard as they progressed through their English classwork. Since instructional practice will also be aligned with the content standards, this alignment creates coherence across instruction, curriculum, and assessment. Webb (1997) provides this definition of curriculum alignment: "the degree to which expectations and assessments are in agreement and serve in conjunction with one another to guide the system toward students learning what they are expected to know and do" (p. 3).

While washback and curriculum alignment tend to carry negative and positive connotations, the term **teaching to the test** is associated with negative consequences or flawed instructional practices. The traditional view is that classroom activities are reduced to a point where teachers focus only on preparing students to answer test questions expected to appear on standardized exams—what Popham (2001) refers to as **item teaching**. The literature reports a wide range of negative consequences for this practice/malpractice (Alderson & Wall, 1993; Cheng, Rogers, & Hu, 2004; Noble & Smith, 1994; Wall, 1997). For example, Noble and Smith (1994) found that while teaching to the test may improve test scores, it is unlikely to help students understand the content of the course. Smith (1991) provides a summary of negative consequences, such as reducing instructional time by focusing on test-preparation exercises, narrowing the scope of the curriculum, and limiting teachers' creativity. As a result, instructional activities stray from didactic teaching to become item teaching.

Different Approaches to Test Preparation

Crocker (2005) laments the bad reputation of test-preparation skills because many teachers think of test preparation as a "tawdry practice. They may avoid it or undertake instruction geared to preparing students to demonstrate their knowledge in a particular format . . . in a shameful or clandestine fashion" (p. 160). In contrast, a more favorable practice that we advocate is **teaching for the test**, which does not involve any narrowing of the curricular scope since it focuses on assessment as an integral part of instruction:

- **Teaching to the test** only focuses on content or skills related to the test.
- **Teaching for the test** considers the preparation of students for exams, but real learning is not ignored (Crocker, 2006). This approach perceives assessment as an important aspect of the learning process and, consequently, is not in a state of conflict with it.

Most teachers are frequently pulled in two directions between testing demands and the fulfillment of curriculum objectives. It may help for teachers to consider differences across various test-preparation activities as some may be more purposeful than others. A study by Lai and Waltman (2008) looked specifically at how K–12 teachers judge test preparation for state-mandated standardized tests. The researchers presented teachers with five test-preparation practices:

1. Practice with the same test questions (as the current test).
2. Practice with last year's questions.
3. Review test content and skills just before testing.
4. Use practice tests.
5. Teach test-taking skills.

Through interviews, 96 teachers were asked to judge these practices as appropriate or inappropriate as well as explain the reasoning behind this choice. The results showed that 100 percent of the teachers felt practicing with the same form of the test (that students would be given) was inappropriate. In contrast, nearly all the teachers (98 percent) cited the practice of teaching test-taking skills as acceptable. According to the teachers in this study, practice with the previous year's test questions was also not good (91 percent judged it inappropriate). Reviewing content areas and skills just before testing had less absolute results: 65 percent said it was appropriate and 37 percent judged it to be inappropriate practice. Using practice tests had mixed results, with 79 percent finding it appropriate and 21 percent as inappropriate.

The researchers also looked at the reasons behind the teachers' judgments and coded them in relation to six categories: professional ethics, negative perception, equity, the importance of learning, score meaning (validity), and likelihood of raising scores. Table 8.1 shows the percentage of times that each of these reasons appeared in teachers' interviews, with a focus on what they considered the most appropriate and inappropriate practices. Teachers thought teaching test-taking skills was appropriate largely because it could help students' learning and

TABLE 8.1: Teachers' Reasons for Opinions on Test-Preparation Activities

	Ethics	Perception	Equity	Learning	Score Meaning	Raise Score
Teaching test-taking skills is appropriate because	0	0	7	80	56	68
Practice with same test items is not appropriate because	56	45	31	59	93	0

improved validity (the scores' meaning). They reasoned that practice with live tests was unacceptable because it affected the validity of scores, did not aid in learning, and was not ethical. This study shows that there is a range in test-preparation activities and that reasons such as validity, learning, and professional ethics can guide teachers' judgment.

Test Preparation and Validity

If we view test preparation from the viewpoint of validity, then it is important for test-takers to perform accurately. (See Myth 6 for a detailed discussion of validity.) This is simply because test questions are used to make inferences about test-takers' abilities. Validity in this sense is related to the concept of access in the context of educational testing (see Myth 7 on access), described as the "opportunity for a student to demonstrate what she or he knows on a test. It is the opportunity to determine how proficient the student is on the target construct . . . and can be conceptualized as an interaction between the individual and the test" (Kettler, Braden, & Beddow, 2011, p. 147). Test preparation is one of the strategies that facilitates access to test materials and consequently improves both the reliability and validity of test scores.

Test-taking strategies can help improve the reliability and validity of test scores by reducing variations in test performance among test-takers (Messick, 1982). We are not referring to variation related to differences in language ability, but rather to factors other than the skills measured on the tests. An example of how test-taking strategies could help reduce such inconsistencies concerns ELLs in U.S. elementary and secondary settings. Because of state and national educational policies, many ELLs are required to regularly take standardized tests in content areas such as Mathematics and Science. The construct of these content tests is not related to language proficiency; however, English reading ability is a factor that can negatively affect test scores. Since the purpose of the tests is not to assess reading ability, its effect on test performance is considered irrelevant to the construct and a source of error. Error refers to the variation in score related to factors other than what is being tested. As ELLs may still be developing second language reading abilities, test-taking strategies focused on helping ELLs approach math or science with reading-related skills would be valuable preparation for these tests. These strategies are expected to help ELLs improve their math and science scores and enhance the validity of these test scores by maximizing the degree to which the assessment results reflect the construct of interest (Math and Science). Here test preparation is not bad because it creates a fairer and more meaningful learning situation.

While test preparation has the potential to improve validity, certain approaches to teaching to the test can have the reverse effect—in particular, approaches that diminish the curriculum in order to focus on test-related topics. A research study by Xie (2013) articulates the two key questions at the core of the relationship between test preparation and validity:

1. Does test preparation inflate scores?
2. If so, to what extent do the inflated scores reflect a corresponding increase on the intended constructs of the test? (p. 196)

Xie explored impact of test preparation on a standardized paper-based test of academic English language proficiency in China that is administered to undergraduates and frequently used for graduation and job screening purposes. The test includes sections on listening, reading, writing, and integrative items (cloze and translation). In Xie's study, a self-report questionnaire and pre-test/post-test were given to 1,000 students to see how often they employed the following six activities in preparing for the test over a ten-week period in their English classes:

- **Test-preparation management:** metacognitive strategies such as reading testing materials and considering one's strengths and weaknesses on practice tests
- **Rehearsing test-taking skills:** trying out different test-taking strategies with practice test items
- **Memorizing:** rote learning of words, phrases, or exemplar responses
- **Drilling:** repetitive practice of focused test-related skills or knowledge
- **Socio-affective strategies:** finding support with teachers or peers, motivation, and anxiety reduction strategies
- **Language skills development:** improving language skills through practice involving the extensive and functional use and practice of authentic English language

Xie (2013) provides evidence that three of these—test-preparation management, memorizing, and drilling—are activities that could narrow the curriculum by creating a negative impact from the test and also interfering with the validity of the test scores. On the other hand, socio-affective strategies, language skills development, and, potentially, rehearsing test-taking skills could improve the representation of the construct in scores, having a positive impact on validity. The frequency of the self-reported activities revealed that language skill development was used the least or "scarcely at all" (p. 205) in the ten weeks prior to taking the test. The other five activities were reported more frequently, with rehearsing test-taking skills as the highest, followed by test-preparation management, drilling, and memorizing. Socio-affective strategies appeared more than language skill development but less than memorizing.

Xie (2013) also discovered that, while test preparation had an impact on score, the effect sizes were small. The activities that narrowed the curriculum had the largest impact, especially drilling, although, again, with a small effect size. The activities related to learning, socio-affective strategies, and rehearsing test-taking skills, had no impact on score. Since language development strategies were scarcely used by these students, we might expect it to have little consequence. This study is useful in considering the different activities involved in test preparation and also shows that their gains are not large. Based on these results, perhaps time is better spent preparing for the life after the test, such as using language for work or academic studies, rather than on test-preparation activities that seem to lead only to minor score improvement.

Test Preparation and Ethics

A question that teachers commonly ask is whether teaching students test-taking strategies is ethical. Kettler et al. (2011) provide an answer to this question using a continuum of test preparation that positions ethical behavior on one end and unethical practice at the other end, as shown in Figure 8.1. Giving general instruction and offering test-taking strategies are considered ethical, but when instruction is narrowed to practicing actual test items, test preparation becomes potentially unethical.

Crocker (2005) also provides a number of criteria for evaluating ethical practices in test preparation, which teachers can use to consider their test preparation activities by asking whether an activity:

- is consistent with ethics of education (no cheating or copying others' work)
- improves validity, which involves exhibiting students' actual ability on the test
- is transferable (i.e., the applicability of test-preparation skills taught in a given context to a wide range of tests)

FIGURE 8.1: Continuum of Ethical Test Preparation

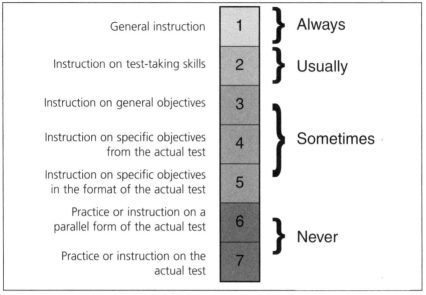

Source: Kettler, Braden, & Beddow (2011), "Test-taking skills and their impact on accessibility for all students," in *Handbook of Accessible Achievement Tests for All Students: Bridging the Gaps between Research, Practice, and Policy,* Springer, p. 152. Used with permission.

- is educationally valuable, meaning that score improvement as a result of test preparation should be indicative of true improvement in the mastery of the target knowledge and skills.

In sum, test preparation is sometimes perceived negatively in educational circles because it may narrow the scope of the curriculum. We need to also consider its relationship with a wide range of variables including validity, educational access, and fairness. Additionally, this approach should conceive of assessment as an integral part of learning. If a test is designed well for a particular setting, it should mesh with the curriculum and goals of that program. In this case, teaching to the test is the same as teaching to the curriculum or to the planned use of the language (Brown, 2008). Our premise is that if the quality of assessment is improved and integrated with learning, it can lead to better execution of curriculum-related decisions, including test preparation.

What We Can Do . . .

Test preparation can be a valuable activity for meaningful integration between assessment and learning; however, teachers and administrators need to be careful not to allow tests alone to drive the curriculum.

1. Teach test-taking strategies.

Students need some preparation before a test so that they are able to perform at their best level, rather than being confused by unexpected formats or overwhelmed by time pressures or anxiety. Before students take a test, a number of activities can be helpful to them as preparation:

- Familiarizing students with the different item formats on the test, such as multiple choice questions, matching, or integrated skills tasks.
- Educating students on processes and strategies used to approach these different item formats.
- Giving students practice answering sample test items.
- Addressing scoring criteria and weight of different test sections.
- Familiarizing students with the general instructions for a test and instructions used with different test sections.
- Teaching students how to pace themselves when taking the test in an allotted time period.

2. Provide all test candidates with access to test-preparation materials or classes.

Access is a fairness issue that can substantially affect both score accuracy and validity (see Myth 7 for a detailed discussion of fairness). Students who come from affluent families sometimes have access to test materials and test-preparation opportunities that other students do not. Deil-Amen and Tevis (2010) found that students coming from lower socio-economic neighborhoods in the U.S. had to rely on their local schools as their main source of information about the ACT® assessment (a college admissions exam). Unfortunately, these schools were unable to provide the quality information that other schools could, which resulted in those students being not as well-prepared as others. Park (2012) also found that "coming from a low-income family decreased the likelihood of SAT® prep" (p. 16). In a recent *New York Times* article (Carrns, 2014), one SAT tutor was reported to charge $1,000 an hour by promising an average increase of 400 points on the total score. In addition, online tutoring was found advertised at $9,000 for a 60-hour test-preparation package. For this reason, it is very important to make sure that all students have access to test-preparation materials regardless of their background. A very good example for making these materials available is in the context of large-scale language proficiency testing, such as TOEFL® and IELTS® tests, where test candidates receive a test-taker's manual when they register for these tests. This manual typically includes information about the test construct, the skills tested, the number of items, the time allotted for each section, and sample items.

3. Develop assessment literacy about test preparation.

Assessment literacy is one of the primary safeguards to ensure sound and ethical test-preparation activities (see Myth 1 for a discussion of assessment literacy). Teachers need to have essential information about what is considered appropriate assessment practice, when and how to teach test-taking strategies, and the variables that affect score validity and interpretation. With the growing pressures on teachers, especially with the accountability policies that hold teachers responsible for the performance of their students on externally mandated and high-stakes tests, low assessment literacy might result in intentional or unintentional unethical practices. Assessment literacy can empower teachers and can help them become active participants in decision-making. Shohamy (2007) advocates that educators assume more responsibility by asking for "greater participation and representation in the decision-making process, decisions not only about what is tested, but how and why" (p. 529). While teachers do not have control over decisions related to externally mandated testing, assessment literacy can help them better prepare their students for these exams and also adequately interpret and use assessment results.

4. Educate the stakeholders.

School administrators and parents want their students/children to perform well on standardized exams. Park (2012), referring to immigrants in the United States, argues that these families look at education to provide social mobility and are therefore willing to sacrifice for their children's success in school. High-stakes exams are often considered the main indicator for this success, leading parents to seek coaching and teaching-to-the-test activities to prepare their sons and daughters for these exams, as was illustrated in the newspaper article about *thanaweya amma* (Leila, 2012).

Students also seek to help from teachers to prepare for tests, sometimes with approaches unlikely to promote long-term learning, such as memorizing or decontextualized drilling. Cheng and DeLuca (2011) collected written responses from 59 test-takers to this prompt:

> Write a report of a real-life language testing event in which you participated as a test-taker. Your report should be a reflection on your positive, neutral, or negative experience with the language test and should address an issue of test validity and test use. Your report should be approximately 300–500 words in length. (p. 108)

They analyzed the responses for emerging themes related to test validity such as test structure, test administration, or psychological factors. Of the eight themes discovered, test preparation was the most frequently mentioned by test-takers (21 times), closely followed by psychological factors (20), which were mostly related to anxiety and negative emotions, and then by test structure and content (20). Within the theme of test preparation, test-takers wrote about the effects of test preparation and the beneficial or detrimental effects of the alignment of test preparation and the actual test format. When the authors looked to see what themes were overlapping in test-takers' responses, they found test preparation was frequently appearing in the same response with comments about test administration, test content, and test purpose. It also co-occurred with psychological factors, which may be related to lowering anxiety through preparation. The results of this study indicate that in the minds of test-takers, test preparation is an integral part of the test-taking process, which test-takers relate to the concept of validity and test use. Since students are focused on test preparation, teachers can educate them on the different approaches, providing guidance in strategies and knowledge that contribute to a test's construct. Teachers should also point out practices that negatively impact the scores and validity, emphasizing the subsequent consequences of an inflated score, such as entering programs unprepared for their language demands, which leads to stress and possible failure.

Last, school administrators might feel forced to employ teaching to the test, especially when their schools are on a watch list because of poor performance on mandated tests. Parents, school administrators, and other stakeholders should be educated about appropriate test-preparation practices and also should understand the serious consequences of teaching to the test. Teachers have a role to play in this process by discussing these ideas in their meetings with parents or other stakeholders.

5. Uphold professional standards.

Teachers, test developers, and policymakers should strive to uphold high standards and codes of ethics that ensure appropriate assessment practices. One highly regarded professional code in educational testing/language assessment is the *Standards for Educational and Psychological Testing*, which was jointly published, most recently in 2014, by the American Educational Research Association (AERA), the American Psychological Association (APA), and the National Council

FIGURE 8.2: Sample Standards

Standard 4.16. Test Design and Development

The instructions presented to test-takers should contain sufficient detail so that test takers can respond to a task in the manner that the test developer intended. When appropriate, sample materials, practice or sample questions, criteria for scoring, and a representative item identified with each item or major area in the test's classification or domain should be provided to the test-takers prior to the administration of the test, or should be included in the testing material as part of the standard administration instructions. (AERA, APA, & NCME, 2014, p. 90)

Standard 8.1. The Rights and Responsibilities of Test-Takers

Information about test content and purposes that is available to any test-taker should be available to all test-takers. Shared information should be available free of charge and in accessible formats. (AERA, APA, & NCME, 2014, p. 133)

Standard 8.2. The Rights and Responsibilities of Test-Takers

Test-takers should be provided in advance with as much information about the test, the testing process, the intended test use, test scoring criteria, testing policy, availability of accommodations, and confidentiality protection as is consistent with obtaining valid responses and making appropriate interpretations of test scores. (AERA, APA, & NCME, 2014, p. 134)

Standard 12.7. Educational Testing and Assessment

In educational settings, test users should take steps to prevent test-preparation activities and distribution of materials to students that might adversely affect the validity of test score inferences. (AERA, APA, & NCME, 2014, p. 197)

on Measurement in Education (NCME). This document includes guidelines that address a wide range of test-preparation issues, such as coaching, appropriate practice materials, expected test performance, and test-takers' access to test-preparation materials. Because it is important that different stakeholders be informed about these standards to make sure that their assessment practices are in accordance with professional guidelines, some samples are listed in Figure 8.2.

A number of other documents provide professional guidelines for those working in the assessment field. Consider consulting the ILTA Code of Ethics & Code of Practice (developed by the International

Language Testing Association, 2007), the Code of Fair Testing Practices (Joint Committee on Testing Practices, 2004), and the National Council on Measurement in Education Code of Professional Responsibilities (NCME, 1995). All of these documents can be found on the associated organization's website.

Conclusion

This book has considered a range of myths held about language assessment, has explored how research has investigated each, and has provided language teachers with suggestions for practice. Assessment is a critical part of instruction and, for better or worse, has transformative power over education. Teachers have a responsibility to follow positive assessment practices and stave off misuse and misinterpretation of tests. We hope through frank discussion of each myth, teachers can see their pivotal role in the assessment process from writing and using tests to negotiating the impact of tests on their students and classrooms.

About the Myths Included in This Book

What teachers need to learn about testing-related language instruction was the topic for Myth 1. Recently, the issue of assessment literacy has garnered attention in research, although teacher education has been grappling with defining this domain for some time. While teacher education programs attempt to develop assessment skills among prospective and in-service teachers, the outcomes are not always satisfactory. This was illustrated in a study by Jeong (2011), which collected data from in-service teachers on assessment literacy and concluded that teachers' assessment knowledge was mainly acquired through trial and error rather than through training courses. There is a great deal for teachers to learn about assessment, and they need to have the flexibility, intuition, and confidence to deal with the many issues that come up surrounding assessments in their classrooms and those mandated by administrators and politicians. Teachers need to recognize the important role assessment plays in their professional development and seek ways to stay abreast of this area of instruction. Hopefully, this book, among others, aids in the development of assessment literacy and promote opportunities for discussions among teachers about appropriate assessment practices. We believe that open discussion among practitioners is one of the main outlets for professional development and for reforming inappropriate instructional activities.

Myth 2 delves into formative assessment and ways to integrate assessment coherently into the curriculum and lesson plans of language classes. Several approaches from general education have been adapted for language teaching, namely Dynamic Assessment and Assessment for Learning, which have provided research and practice to guide teachers in implementing assessment that is individually focused and involves students in their development. This new trend is much needed in an age where accountability-driven assessment tools are increasingly used in schools worldwide. In such contexts, externally mandated tests have often created an unfortunate tension between instruction and assessment. Teachers are in the position of having to juggle with competing priorities and often feel forced to spend class time on irrelevant activities to satisfy accountability requirements.

Attention to classroom-based assessment in the field of language testing will likely help teachers ease the tension between instruction and assessment by providing more approaches to elevate and integrate assessment into the language classrooms. The Assessment Reform Group (ARG, 2002) articulates ten principles for effective Assessment for Learning in classrooms. ARG says that assessment should:

1. be part of effective planning of teaching and learning.
2. focus on how students learn.
3. be central to classroom practice.
4. be a key professional skill for teachers.
5. be sensitive and constructive because assessment has an emotional impact.
6. take account of the importance of learner motivation.
7. promote commitment to learning goals and assessment criteria.
8. ensure that learners receive constructive guidance about how to improve.

9. develop the leaner's capacity for self-assessment so that he or she can become reflective and self-managing.

10. recognize the full range of achievements of all students.

Performance assessment is the topic of Myth 3, which challenged this method of testing language use, not in its overall importance, but in the many aspects that can derail the meaningfulness of scores of such tests. Teachers embrace performance assessment because of its authenticity; it visibly shows how a student can (or cannot) use language. However, the procedures in conducting and scoring performance assessments require careful consideration. Teachers need to design performance tasks that are clear to test-takers and concurrently similar to real-life language situations.

While the design of good tasks is important, as much time should be spent contemplating the scoring of performance assessments. Scoring rubrics for performance assessment tasks are especially efficacious in this respect, and teachers should be prepared to develop their own scoring rubrics in case appropriate tools are not available. A wide range of resources is available on the Internet and in assessment books on how to develop scoring rubrics. If teachers work as a team when scoring performance tasks, group discussions can clarify how each teacher conceptualizes the rubric descriptors. Linking a rubric's level descriptors to sample tasks provides meaningful training for teachers on how to utilize the rubric in scoring performance assessment. These procedures can help teachers overcome some of the missteps encountered during scoring performances on speaking and writing activities. Teachers should consider creative approaches to convey scoring criteria to students before and after a task; the insight into criteria can lead student to perform better and to meet the expectations of their teachers. More important, engaging students with scoring rubrics results in positive washback in language classes by raising awareness of the standards for language proficiency and by encouraging students to work toward reaching these levels.

Myth 4 continues with the theme of methodology in language testing, presenting the maligned multiple choice question. This form of test question has been a mainstay in testing, providing either dismay or relief in teachers and test-takers. In our language testing courses, student-led discussion often turns to criticisms of multiple choice questions on large-scale tests, which inspired us to address the topic in this book. In many cases, particularly in classroom assessments, these questions are not appropriate for assessment of learning or development. However, well-designed multiple choice questions can improve the precision of a measure and yield efficient qualities that are important in testing. Tests can have many more multiple choice questions than performance assessment tasks, thus tapping into a wider range of skills and language features. The potential these items have for comprehensive coverage of a curriculum may improve a test's content-related validity by ensuring that the test questions are representative of the breadth of content from language classes.

In essence, the problem lies not with the MCQs per se but with their design and development. Multiple choice question development requires careful construction and piloting to prevent bias and promote differentiation, making them one of the most challenging types of questions to write, not the easiest. Writing good and effective MCQs is a necessary skill for teachers. Since programs that develop their own tests for placement will likely include multiple choice questions, this chapter provides guidance on writing good questions. In addition, comprehending the process and procedures for designing such items can help teachers consider how and why they supply useful information in large-scale tests. Teachers should be familiar with these procedures to ensure the quality of MCQs produced and employed in their context.

This chapter also briefly touched on some technical aspects related to assessing the difficulty of MCQs and determining whether a MCQ discriminates well among students at different proficiency levels. Also highlighted are unfavorable test-wiseness activities that students may try when answering MCQ questions. Teachers should be aware of these detrimental practices and strive to prevent their negative washback and thus improve score interpretation and use of MCQ items.

In Myth 5, the view of language as four separate skills is broached, and an alternative perspective, one that espouses the integration of skills, is proposed. Integrating skills reflects the way language commonly occurs in academic, social, and professional contexts where skills are rarely utilized independently. This approach to language assessment enhances the authenticity of test tasks and taps into holistic language ability. While many benefits are gained from using integrated tasks, a host of challenges emerge, including task design, scoring, and other validity-related dilemmas. These need careful consideration by teachers when developing integrated skills tasks or interpreting the results from such tasks. A common challenge for students and teachers employing these tasks is how to successfully achieve discourse synthesis in integration. Students may rely too much on external sources in their writing or employ other inappropriate textual borrowing practices. Guided practice with instruction in class is critical for building strategies for integrating language skills.

Validity is commonly considered when evaluating tests, and Myth 6 attempts to clarify the meaning of this term, based on current theory in language testing, with relevance to teachers. This chapter reviewed a number of views of validity and approaches to investigating it. Given the impact of decisions made by language teachers, program administrators, and other test users, validity is a critical issue to consider in the development and use of assessments. An understanding of the essence of validity is required, along with deliberate planning and reflection on validity evidence in testing practices. Teachers need to articulate the purpose for their assessments and ensure that tests align with the curriculum they are teaching. They can improve the validity in decision-making by collecting multiple measures when assessing students for major decisions and critiquing all measures thoughtfully. In-house tests need to be monitored and revised regularly to assure the results can be interpreted and used appropriately.

While the details of validity have evolved over the years, its importance in assessment has not. We hope that this chapter will encourage language professionals to engage in constructive discussions about different validity aspects in their local assessment contexts. In these discussions, a number of validity issues are relevant, including why a specific test is needed, what its purpose is, how the test content is related to this purpose and to the target language use context, how the test is scored and what criteria should be employed, and finally how a score obtained from this test will be interpreted and used. These issues are relevant in any assessment context, whether a large-scale test or a classroom assessment. Knowledge of such issues facilitates teachers' development of good assessment tools and leads to professionally sound decisions based on their results.

Myth 7 addresses the very serious issue of fairness, which has motivated testing but also has been exacerbated by testing. This chapter elucidates some of the misconceptions about fairness by revealing approaches in large-scale assessment to measure bias. For language testing, fairness is a significant issue in test development and administration given the increasing diversity in students and test-takers worldwide. Fairness includes considering the cultural and background knowledge embedded in the content of our assessments as well as formats that may be unfamiliar to students. Fairness is about giving all students the opportunity to show their best language skills through our assessments and to leverage those opportunities as venues for learning. This chapter describes a number of established professional guidelines and practices that can promote fair test development and use. The chapter also raises awareness about the differences in test performance that are due to unfair practices and those due to limited opportunities to learn. Judgments of fairness involve understanding and interpreting how test scores are affected by different variables. For this reason, teachers need to look into fairness issues from various perspectives. Teachers should also carefully inspect test items for potential issues that might cause bias. Procedures to check bias described in the chapter could be useful in alleviating its impact on test scores.

Myth 8 discusses the hot-button topic of teaching to the test. Test preparation is generally perceived negatively in educational circles and often accused of narrowing the curricular scope. However, the potential for good also exists in test preparation, and it cannot be dismissed wholesale when considering its relationship with a wide range of variables including validity, educational access, and fairness. If a test is designed thoughtfully for a particular setting, it should mesh with the curriculum and goals for learning. In this case, teaching for the test is the same as teaching for the curriculum or for the planned use of the language (Brown, 2008). Following the same argument, Messick (1996) argues that the "move from learning exercises to test exercises should be seamless" (p. 24). Consequently, we should not see substantial differences between test-preparation activities and regular instructional tasks in language classes. This chapter also reviewed unethical test-preparation activities that teachers should avoid, such as giving students active test items to practice or focusing a course wholly on developing test-wiseness. Such practices diminish not only fairness, but also the validity of test scores because test performance will be confounded by variables irrelevant to language ability.

About the Myths Left on the Cutting Room Floor

This book was not written to detail every aspect of language testing but to cover certain issues that have been misconstrued or misunderstood. Some myths overlap with general language testing topics, such as performance assessment, validity, or formative assessment, but the format of this book allows us to address some issues not commonly found in textbooks, such as teaching to the test. In conceptualizing the book, several myths could not be included. These were myths that we are aware of and felt needed debate, but as we reviewed the research, we found that they were understudied. While the topics have been discussed in the field and, in some cases, position papers or presentations have addressed them, we did not find research that unarguably disproves them. The myths may be of relevance and interest to teachers, so we are mentioning them here. They may also be seen as research areas, as the field would benefit from empirical studies to reject or confirm the myths.

• *Myth: Commercially designed tests are better than teacher-designed tests.* We have both been perplexed in meetings where teachers chose textbooks specifically because they included test banks. The sentiment prevails that a test or quiz from a published source is better than a teacher-created test; however, we feel that if teachers have assessment literacy, they are likely to design tests more appropriate to their students' language ability. The knowledge teachers bring to the testing process is invaluable: familiarity with course content, background knowledge about the students taking the test, a vision of how the test informs decisions in class and about students, and knowledge of the time and resources available for implementing a test. Our preference is to first look to teachers for classroom assessment development and then to include commercial materials as needed. However, to our dismay, little research has tackled the topic of teacher-developed versus commercially produced assessments. However, a few studies have found that rubrics developed by teachers can have a positive impact on the testing process (Plakans, 2013; Turner, 2000). In-depth study of teacher-created assessments could certainly add to our knowledge of how key stakeholders—teachers—affect the development of assessments.

• *Myth: Students' language should only be assessed by the teacher.* This myth was eventually collapsed into other chapters, such as the section on Assessment for Learning in Myth 2 and rubric development in Myth 3. However, initially we wished to address the belief often held by teachers and students that useful feedback can only come from the teacher. In the teaching of writing, the practice of peer review has become routine, and research has shown its productive impact (Cheng & Wang, 2007). Self-assessment is also a practice introduced in teaching to promote reflection and self-awareness and has also appeared more readily in writing instruction than with other skills. However, with both peer and self-assessment, great care is needed in implementation for the results to be productive. The myth may be credible if peer or self-assessment is enacted without proper introduction, implementation, and follow up. For this reason, it made more sense to us to contextualize these topics within specific practices. However, using teacher, peer, and self-assessment in concert is recommended for classroom assessment practice.

• *Myth: The most valid way to assess language is through a test.* In this myth, we wished to address what have been called "alternative assessments," which includes a wide range of evaluative activities, such as observations or learner portfolios. The general thrust in most assessment is to elicit numerical data on which to make inferences about language ability; however, we can easily lose valuable information about learners in this operationalization. Therefore, collecting performances and process-related samples of students' work should also be considered in evaluation of learning to capture a rounded profile of an individual student. Looking into the research in this area was tricky because we stated the myth as a comparison to tests, which is not necessary because both approaches to assessment provide useful and valid information about learners. Studies have presented information on portfolios and other assessments, but not in contrast to tests. While we know that alternative assessments are as informative as tests, the prevailing myth pits the two approaches to assessment against each other when they really should work together.

• *Myth: Technology has made language testing better.* The discussion of the impact of technology on many fields seems to boil down to whether it has been evolutionary or revolutionary. Practicality, fairness, or security issues temper enthusiasm for technology, particularly in assessment. However, it has played an important role in providing more convenient, realistic, and efficient testing. Innovation has emerged, but slowly and with the continued appearance of items that we associate with paper-based testing, such as multiple choice questions (Chapelle & Douglas, 2006). When we started exploring the research on this topic in the field of language assessment, despite many publications on computer-based testing (CBT) in language learning, we felt a lack of clear consensus for or against the myth. Again, perhaps the wording was too simple for a topic so large. In any case, we decided that it was not within the scope of this book to take a stance on technology's impact on language assessment.

Future Directions for Assessment in Research and Teacher Education

The myths not included in this book present areas needing more research, but it became clear to us that other issues also require future research. For example, research that investigates how teachers successfully integrate assessment and instruction would enhance our wisdom of how context, learners, and teachers interact in educational settings. This knowledge can help us go beyond general or abstract suggestions to actual paths in decision-making and use. Such research could perhaps best be carried out by teachers in their own classrooms using approaches such as participatory action research (Burns, 2010), which entails systematic study of one's own setting. This type of research is very important in exploring how assessment is perceived and implemented in classroom contexts and will definitely fill in a gap in the literature. Generally, much of the published research in the area of language assessment is either carried out in large-scale test contexts and/or by language testing researchers who do not work regularly in schools. Involving teachers in this line of research would enrich research efforts and would add to our existing knowledge about the field. Burns (2010) suggested four steps for action research in schools:

- planning the suggested project
- putting the plan into action
- observing the results of the plan
- reflecting on the process and planning for further action.

Following these basic steps could assist teachers in carrying out successful action research projects to explore how assessment functions within their local contexts.

In addition to the study of classroom assessment by teachers, language programs' attention to test use will increase insight into best practices and procedures. Again, self-study is a productive and reflective way to research tests in practice, which feeds into program evaluation and program improvement. It requires teams of teachers working along with program administrators to collect useful data and analyze it for research questions important to the program.

Another area to explore further is teachers' and students' perceptions of assessment and their beliefs about how it impacts their learning. Approaches such as Assessment for Learning or peer review advocate for substantial involvement by teachers and students in the evaluation process. Such learner-centered assessment benefits from collecting candid data from students and teachers on their views about classroom assessment. In fact, learners may have very astute observations on how to best display their knowledge and what feedback supports their improvement. Surveys with students or activities in which they design assessments can give teachers and researchers insight into the learners' perspectives on testing. Data collected from teachers about their conceptions of assessment can also help inform policies in schools. The scarcity of research in this area has shown that the way teachers conceive of assessment can substantially affect the implementation of policies (Gebril & Brown, 2014).

A main point repeatedly stressed in this book is that assessment wields a great deal of power over teachers and students. This trend seems to be continuing without adequately listening to the stakeholders involved. Assessment-driven educational systems may in fact be driving people away from becoming teachers, given the perceived focus on tests in education. Our field has two responsibilities in this struggle. One is to ensure that assessment is aligned to learning and development rather than being punitive or gate-keeping. The other is to advocate for this balance and critique overzealous assessment endeavors that may derail the intent of teachers for their students. Learning should remain the dominant process in the classroom rather than the assessment of learning. By recommending such a model, we are not ignoring the larger evaluative functions of assessment. Such data can be useful for informing policymakers and taxpayers about whether the educational system is meeting their expectations. However, this function of assessment should not distract our attention from the real purpose behind learning: development. Our classroom assessments should be utilized in collecting data that can inform instruction and plan for future directions. A test score cannot successfully achieve these objectives alone. Different types of assessment tools should be considered to gather evidence about learning and teaching in classes. For this paradigm to be successful, teachers should have adequate assessment literacy. Assessment literacy is a first step toward learning-friendly assessment.

References

Abbott, M. L. (2007). A confirmatory approach to differential item functioning on an ESL reading assessment. *Language Testing, 24*(1), 7–36.

Abedi, J., & Herman, J. (2010). Assessing English language learners' opportunity to learn mathematics: Issues and limitations. *The Teachers College Record, 112*(3), 723–746.

Alderson, C., & Wall, D. (1993). Does washback exist? *Applied Linguistics, 14*(2), 115–129.

American Council on the Teaching of Foreign Languages. (2012). *ACTFL proficiency guidelines.* White Plains, NY: ACTFL.

American Educational Research Association (AERA), American Psychological Association (APA), & National Council on Measurement in Education (NCME). (2014). *Standards for educational and psychological testing.* Washington, DC: AERA, APA, & NCME.

American Federation of Teachers, National Council on Measurement in Education, and National Education Association. (1990). *Teacher competence in educational assessment of students.* Retrieved from www.unl.edu/buros/bimm/html/article3.html.

Assessment Reform Group. (2002). *Assessment for Learning: 10 Principles.* Retrieved from www.aaia.org.uk/afl/assessment-reform-group/

Bachman, L. F. (1988). Problems in examining the validity of the ACTFL Oral Proficiency Interview. *Studies in Second Language Acquisition, 10,* 149–161.

Bachman, L. F. (2004). *Statistical analyses for language assessment.* Cambridge, U.K.: Cambridge University Press.

Bachman, L. F., & Savignon, S. J. (1986). The evaluation of communicative language proficiency: A critique of the ACTFL Oral Interview. *Modern Language Journal, 69,* 129–142.

Bachman, L. F., & Palmer, A. (1996). *Language testing in practice.* Oxford, U.K.: Oxford University Press.

Banerjee, J., & Wall, D. (2006). Assessing and reporting performances on pre-sessional EAP courses: Developing a final assessment checklist and investigating its validity. *Journal of English for Academic Purposes, 5,* 50–69.

Barkaoui, K. (2011). Effects of marking method and rater experience on ESL essay scores and rater performance. *Assessment in Education: Principles, Policies, and Practice, 18,* 279–293.

Black, P., Harrison, C., Lee, C., Marshall, B., & Williams, D. (2003). *Assessment for learning: Putting it into practice.* Buckingham, U.K.: Open University Press.

Broussard, M. (2014, July 15). Why poor schools can't win at standardized tests. *The Atlantic.* Retrieved from www.theatlantic.com/featuresf/archive/2014/07/why-poor-schools-cant-win-at-standardized-testing/374287/

Brown, A. (1995). The effect of rater variables in the development of an occupation-specific language performance test. *Language Testing, 12,* 1–15.

Brown, J. D. (2008). Testing-context analysis: Assessment is just another part of language curriculum development. *Language Assessment Quarterly, 5*(4), 275–312.

Brown, J. D., & Bailey, K. M. (1996). Language testing courses: What are they? In A. Cumming & R. Berwick (Eds.), *Validation in language testing* (pp. 236–256). Clevedon, U.K.: Multilingual Matters.

Brown, J. D., & Bailey, K. M. (2008). Language testing courses: What are the in 2007? *Language Testing, 25*(3), 349–383.

Burnett, S. (2001). *Myths of global warming.* Retrieved from http://www.ncpa.org/ba/ba230.html

Burns, A. (2010). *Doing action research in English language teaching: A guide for practitioners.* New York: Routledge.

Camili, G. (2006). Test fairness. In R.L. Brennan (Ed.), *Educational measurement* (4th ed.) (pp. 221–256). Westport, CT: Praeger.

Canale, M. (1983). From communicative competence to communicative language pedagogy. In J. C. Richards & R. W. Schmidt (Eds.), *Language and communication* (pp. 2–27). New York: Longman.

Canale, M., & Swain, M. (1980). The theoretical bases of communicative approaches to second language teaching and testing. *Applied Linguistics, 1*, 1–47.

Carrns, A. (2014, October 28). Another college expense: Preparing for the SAT and ACT. *New York Times.* Retrieved from www.nytimes.com/2014/10/29/your-money/another-college-expense-preparing-for-the-sat-and-act-.html?_r=0

Carson, J. (2001). A task analysis of reading and writing in academic contexts. In D. Belcher & A. Hirvela (Eds.), *Linking literacies: Perspectives on L2 reading-writing connections* (pp. 246–270). Ann Arbor: University of Michigan Press.

Central Agency for Public Mobilization and Statistics (CAPMAS)—Egypt. (2013). *Indicators of income, expenditure, and consumptions.* Retrieved from http://capmas.gov.eg/pdf/studies/pdf/enf2012.pdf

Chalhoub–Deville, M. (1995). Deriving oral assessment scales across different tests and rater groups. *Language Testing, 12*, 16–33.

Chalhoub-Deville, M., & Fulcher, G. (2003). The oral proficiency interview and the ACTFL Guidelines: A research agenda. *Foreign Language Annals, 36*, 498–506.

Chapelle, C. (1999). Validity in language assessment. *Annual Review of Applied Linguistics, 19*, 254–272.

Chapelle, C. (2012). Conceptions of validity. In G. Fulcher & F. Davidson (Eds.), *Routledge handbook of language testing.* (pp. 21–33). New York: Routledge.

Chapelle, C. A., & Douglas, D. (2006). *Assessing language through computer technology.* Cambridge, U.K.: Cambridge University Press.

Chapelle, C., Enright, J. M., & Jamieson, J. (2008). *Building a validity argument for the Test of English as a Foreign Language.* New York: Routledge.

Cheng, L., & DeLuca, C. (2011). Voices from test-takers: Further evidence for language assessment validity and use. *Educational Assessment, 16*, 104–122.

Cheng, L., Rogers, T., & Hu, H. (2004). ESL/EFL instructors' classroom assessment practice: Purposes, methods, and procedures. *Language Testing, 21,* 360–389.

Cheng, L., & Wang, X. (2007). Grading, feedback, and reporting in ESL/EFL classrooms. *Language Assessment Quarterly, 4*(1), 85–107.

Cheng, L., Watanabe, Y. J., & Curtis, A. (Eds.). (2004). *Washback in language testing: Research contexts and methods.* Mahwah, NJ: Lawrence Erlbaum.

Cohen, A. D. (1994). *Assessing language ability in the classroom* (2nd ed.). Boston: Newbury House/Heinle & Heinle.

Colby-Kelly, C., & Turner, C. E. (2007). AFL research in the L2 classroom and evidence of usefulness: Taking formative assessment to the next level. *Canadian Modern Language Review, 64*(1), 9–37.

Cole, N. S., & Zieky, M. J. (2001). The new faces of fairness. *Journal of Educational Measurement, 38*(4), 369–382.

Cooper, R. L. (1965). Testing. In H. B. Allen & R. N. Allen (Eds.), *Teaching English as a second language: A book of readings.* New York: McGraw-Hill.

Council of Europe. (2011). *Common European Framework of Reference for languages: Learning, teaching, assessment.* Retrieved from www.coe.int/t/dg4/education/elp/elpreg/Source/Key_reference/CEFR_EN.pdf

Crocker, L. (2005). Teaching for the test: How and why test preparation is appropriate. In R. Phelps (Ed.), *Defending standardized testing* (pp. 159–174). Mahwah, NJ: Lawrence Erlbaum.

Crocker, L. (2006). Preparing examinees for test taking: Guidelines for test developers and test users. In S. Downing & T. Haladyna (Eds.), *Handbook of test development* (pp. 115–128). Mahwah, NJ: Lawrence Erlbaum.

Cronbach, L. (1988). Five perspectives on validity argument. In H. Wainer & H. Braun (Eds.), *Test validity* (pp. 3–17). Hillsdale, NJ: Lawrence Erlbaum.

Cumming, A. (2014). Assessing integrated skills. In A. Kunnan (Ed.), *Companion to language assessment* (pp. 216–229). Malden, MA: Wiley-Blackwell.

Data Recognition Corporation. (2003). *Manual for issues of bias, fairness, and sensitivity.* Retrieved from www.eed.state.ak.us/tls/assessment/TechReports/Spring12_SBA/Sp12SBA_App4.pdf

Davies, A., Brown, A., Elder, C., Hill, K., Lumley, T., & McNamara, T. (1999). *Dictionary of language testing.* Cambridge, U.K.: Cambridge University Press.

Davison, C. (2004). The contradictory culture of teacher-based assessment: ESL teacher assessment practices in Australia and Hong Kong secondary schools. *Language Testing, 21,* 305–334.

Deil-Amen, R., & Tevis, T. L. (2010). Circumscribed agency: The relevance of standardized college entrance exams for low SES high school students. *The Review of Higher Education, 33,* 140–170.

Downing, S. (2006). Selected-response item formats in test development. In S. Downing & T. Haladyna (Eds.), *Handbook of test development* (pp. 287–301). Mahwah, NJ: Lawrence Erlbaum.

Earl, L. M., & Katz, M. S. (2006). *Rethinking classroom assessment with purpose in mind: Assessment for learning, assessment as learning, assessment of learning.* Manitoba, SK: Manitoba Education, Citizenship & Youth.

Eblen, C. (1983). Writing across the curriculum: A survey of a university faculty's views and classroom practices. *Research on the Teaching of English, 17,* 343–349.

Educational Testing Service. (2009). *ETS guidelines for fairness review of assessments.* Princeton, NJ: ETS.

Elder, C. (2013). Bias in language assessment. In Carol Chapelle (Ed.), *Encyclopedia of applied linguistics* (pp. 1–8). New York: Wiley.

Ellery, K. (2008). Assessment for learning: A case study using feedback effectively in an essay-style test. *Assessment & Evaluation in Higher Education, 33,* 421–429.

Fayer, J. M., & Krasinski, E. (1987). Native and non-native judgments of intelligibility and irritation. *Language Learning, 37,* 313–326.

Ferris, D., & Tagg, T. (1996). Academic oral communication needs of EAP learners: What subject-matter instructors actually require. *TESOL Quarterly, 30,* 31–58.

Fitzgerald, J., & Shanahan, T. (2000). Reading and writing relations and their development. *Educational Psychologist, 35,* 39–50.

Fulcher, G. (1996). Invalidating validity claims for the ACTFL oral rating scale. *System, 24,* 163–172.

Fulcher, G. (2010). *Practical language testing.* London: Hodder Education.

Fulcher, G. (2012). Assessment literacy for the language classroom. *Language Assessment Quarterly, 9,* 113–132.

Gebril, A. (2009). Score generalizability of academic writing tasks: Does one test method fit it all? *Language Testing, 26*(4), 507–531.

Gebril, A. (2010). Bringing reading-to-write and writing-only assessment tasks together: A generalizability analysis. *Assessing Writing, 15*(2), 100–117.

Gebril, A., & Brown, G. T. (2014). The effect of high-stakes examination systems on teacher beliefs: Egyptian teachers' conceptions of assessment. *Assessment in Education: Principles, Policy & Practice, 21*(1), 16–33.

Gebril, A., & Plakans, L. (2009). Investigating source use, discourse features, and process in integrated writing tests. *Spaan Fellow Working Papers in Second/Foreign Language Assessment 7* (pp. 47–84). Ann Arbor: University of Michigan.

Gebril A., & Plakans, L. (2013). Towards a transparent construct of reading-to-write assessment tasks: The interface between discourse features and proficiency. *Language Assessment Quarterly, 10*(1), 1–19.

Gipps, C. (1999). Socio-cultural aspects of assessment. In A. Iran-Nejad & P. D. Pearson (Eds.), *Review of research in education* (pp. 355–392). Washington, DC: AERA.

Grabe, W. (1986). The transition from theory to practice in teaching reading. In F. Dublin, D. Eskey, & W. Grabe (Eds.), *Teaching second language reading for academic purposes* (pp. 25–48). New York: Prentice Hall.

Hale, G., Taylor, C., Bridgeman, J., Carson, J., Kroll, B., & Kantor, R. (1996). *A study of writing tasks assigned in academic degree programs* (TOEFL RR-54). Princeton, NJ: ETS.

Hamp-Lyons L., & Zhang B. W. (2001). World Englishes: Issues in and from academic writing assessment. In J. Flowerdew & M. Peacock (Eds.), *Research perspectives on English for academic purposes* (pp.101–116). Cambridge, U.K.: Cambridge University Press.

Hill, K. (1996). Who should be the judge? The use of non-native speakers as raters on a test of English as an international language. *Melbourne Papers in Language Testing, 5*, 29–49.

Horowitz, D. (1986). What professors actually require: Academic tasks for the ESL classroom. *TESOL Quarterly, 20*, 445–462.

Huang, H., & Hung, C. (2010). Examining the practice of a reading-to-speak test task: Anxiety and experience of EFL students. *Asia Pacific Education Review, 11*, 235–242.

Hymes, D. H. (1972). On communicative competence. In J. B. Pride & J. Holmes (Eds.), *Sociolinguistics* (pp. 269–293). Baltimore: Penguin Education.

Inbar-Lourie, O. (2008). Constructing a language assessment knowledge base: A focus on language assessment courses. *Language Testing, 25*, 385–402.

Inbar-Lourie, O. (2013). Guest editorial to the special issues on language assessment literacy. *Language Testing, 30*, 301–307.

International Language Testing Association. (2007). *ILTA code of ethics.* Retrieved from http://www.iltaonline.com/images/pdfs/ILTA_Code.pdf

Jeong, H. (2011). *Perspectives of language assessment training for teachers and testing professionals.* Unpublished doctoral dissertation. University of Illinois, Urbana-Champaign,

Jeong, H. (2013). Defining assessment literacy: Is it different for language testers and non-language testers? *Language Testing, 30*(3), 345–362.

Johns, A. M., & Mayes, P. (1990). An analysis of summary protocols of university ESL students. *Applied Linguistics, 11*(3), 253–271.

Joint Committee on Testing Practices. (2004). Code of fair testing practices in education. Retrieved from http://ncme.org/linkservid/991A492D-1320-5CAE 6E971C543DE4CA6D/showMeta/0/

Kane, M. (2006). Content-related validity evidence in test development. In S. Downing & T. Haladyna (Eds.), *Handbook of test development* (pp. 131–153). Mahwah, NJ: Lawrence Erlbaum.

Kane, M. (2012). Validating score interpretations and use. *Language Testing, 29*, 3–17.

Kane, M., Crooks, T., & Cohen, A. (1999). Validating measures of performance. *Educational Measurement: Issues and Practice, 18*(2), 5–17.

Kettler, R. J., Braden, J. P., & Beddow, P. A. (2011). Test-taking skills and their impact on accessibility for all students. In S. Elliott, R. Kettler, P. Beddow, & A. Kurz (Eds.), *Handbook of accessible achievement tests for all students: Bridging the gaps between research, practice, and policy* (pp. 147–159). New York: Springer.

Kim, Y. (2009). An investigation into native and non-native teachers' judgments of oral English performance: A mixed methods approach. *Language Testing, 26*, 187–217.

Kim, Y., & Jang, E. E. (2009). Differential functioning of reading subskills on the OSSLT for L1 and ELL students: A multidimensionality model-based DBF/DIF approach. *Language Learning, 59*, 825–865.

Knoch, U. (2009). Diagnostic assessment of writing: A comparison of two rating scales, *Language Testing. 26*, 275–304.

Kozulin, A., & Garb, E. (2004). Dynamic assessment of literacy: English as a third language. *European Journal of Psychology of Education, 19*(1), 65–77.

Kuiken, F., Vedder, I., & Gilabert, R. (2010). Communicative adequacy and linguistic complexity in L2 writing. In I. Barting, M. Martin, & I. Vedder (Eds.), *Communicative proficiency and linguistic development: Intersections between SLA and language testing research. EuroSLA Monograph 1* (pp. 81–100). Rome: EuroSLA.

Kunnan, A. (2000). Fairness and justice for all. In A. Kunnan (Ed.), *Fairness and validation in language assessment* (pp. 1–14). Cambridge, U.K.: Cambridge University Press.

Lai, E. R., & Waltman, K. (2008). Test preparation: Examining teacher perceptions and practices. *Educational Measurement: Issues and Practice, 27*, 28–45.

Lantolf, J. P., & Poehner, M. E. (2007). Dynamic assessment of L2 development: Bringing the past into the future. *Journal of Applied Linguistics, 1*(1), 49–72.

Larsen-Freeman, D. (2000). *Techniques and principles in language teaching.* Oxford, U.K.: Oxford University Press.

Lee, I. (2007a). Assessment for learning: Integrating assessment, teaching, and learning in the ESL/EFL writing classroom. *Canadian Modern Language Review, 64*(1), 199–213.

Lee, I. (2007b). Feedback in Hong Kong secondary writing classrooms: Assessment for learning or assessment of learning? *Assessing Writing, 12*(3), 180–198.

Leila, R. (2012, May 9). Test of tests. *Al-Ahram Weekly.* Retrieved from http://weekly.ahram.org.eg/2012/1096/eg17.htm

Leki, I., & Carson, J. (1994). Students' perception of EAP writing instruction and writing across the disciplines. *TESOL Quarterly, 28,* 81–101.

Leki, I., & Carson, J. (1997). "Completely different worlds": EAP and the writing experiences of ESL students in university courses. *TESOL Quarterly, 31,* 39–69.

Leung, C. (2007). Dynamic assessment: Assessment for and as teaching? *Language Assessment Quarterly, 4*(3), 257–278.

Lim, G. (2011). The development and maintenance of rating quality in performance writing assessment: A longitudinal study of experienced and novice raters. *Language Testing, 32,* 543–560.

Liskin-Gasparro, J. (2003). The ACTFL proficiency guidelines and the oral proficiency interview: A brief history and analysis of their survival. *Foreign language Annals, 36,* 483–490.

Lumely, T. (2002). Assessment criteria in a large-scale writing test: What do they really mean to the raters? *Language Testing, 19,* 246–276.

Lumely, T. (2005). *Assessing second language writing: The rater's perspective.* Frankfurt, Germany: Peter Lang.

Malone, M. (2013). The essentials of assesment literacy: Contrasts between testers and users. *Language Testing, 30,* 329–344.

Mehrens, W. A., & Kaminsky, J. (1989). Methods for improving standardized test scores: Fruitful, fruitless or fraudulent? *Educational Measurement: Issues and Practice, 8*(1), 14–22.

McNamara, T., & Roever, C. (2006). *Language testing: The social dimension.* Malden, MA: Blackwell.

Messick, S. (1982). Issues of effectiveness and equity in the coaching controversy: Implications for educational and testing practice. *Educational Psychologist, 17*(2), 67–91.

Messick, S. (1989). Validity. In R.L. Linn (Ed.), *Handbook of educational measurement* (3rd ed.) (pp. 12–103). New York: MacMillan.

Messick, S. (1996). Validity and washback in language testing. *Language Testing, 13*(3), 241–256.

Moore, T., & Morton, J. (1999). *Authenticity in the IELTS academic module writing test: A comparative study of task 2 items and university assignments* (IELTS Research Reports No. 2). Canberra: IELTS Australia.

National Council on Measurement in Education. (1995). *Code of Professional Responsibilities.* Retrieved from http://ncme.org/resource-center/code-of-professional-responsibilities-in-educational-measurement

Noble, A. J., & Smith, M. L. (1994). *Measurement-driven reform: Research on policy, practice, repercussion.* (Technical Report No. 381). Tempe: Arizona State University Center for the Study of Evaluation.

Norris, J. M. (2008). *Validity evaluation in language assessment.* Frankfurt, Germany: Peter Lang.

Oskoz, A. (2005). Students' dynamic assessment via online chat. *Journal CALICO, 22(3)*, 513–536.

Ostler, S. E. (1980). A survey of academic needs for advanced ESL. *TESOL Quarterly, 14*, 489–502.

Pae, T. I., & Park, G. P. (2006). Examining the relationship between differential item functioning and differential test functioning. *Language Testing, 23*(14), 475–496.

Park, J. J. (2012). It takes a village (or an ethnic economy): The varying roles of socioeconomic status, religion, and social capital in SAT preparation for Chinese and Korean American students. *American Educational Research Journal, 49*(4), 624–650.

Pennycook, A. (1996). Borrowing others' words: Text, ownership, memory, and plagiarism. *TESOL Quarterly, 30*(2), 201–230.

Plakans, L. (2008). Comparing composing processes in writing-only and reading-to-write test tasks. *Assessing Writing, 13,* 111–129.

Plakans, L. (2009). Discourse synthesis in integrated second language writing assessment. *Language Testing, 26,* 561–587.

Plakans, L. (2013). Writing scale development and use in a language program. *TESOL Journal, 4,* 151–163.

Plakans, L., & Gebril, A. (2012). A close investigation into source use in L2 integrated writing tasks. *Assessing Writing, 17*(1), 18–34.

Plakans, L., & Gebril, A. (2013). Using multiple texts in an integrated writing assessment: Source text use as a predictor of score. *Journal of Second Language Writing, 22,* 217–230.

Poehner, M. E. (2007). Beyond the test: L2 dynamic assessment and the transcendence of mediated learning. *Modern Language Journal, 91*(3), 323–340.

Poehner, M. E. (2008). *Dynamic assessment: A Vygotskian approach to understanding and promoting L2 development.* New York: Springer.

Poehner, M. E. (2009). Group dynamic assessment: Mediation for the L2 classroom. *TESOL Quarterly, 43*(30), 471–491.

Poehner, M. E., & Compernolle, R. A. (2011). Frames of interaction in dynamic assessment: Developmental diagnoses of second language learning. *Assessment in Education: Principles, Policy & Practice, 18*(2), 183–198.

Poehner, M. E., & Lantolf, J. P. (2005). Dynamic assessment in the language classroom. *Language Teaching Research, 9*(3), 233–265.

Popham, W. J. (2001). Teaching to the test? *Educational Leadership, 58*(6), 16–21.

Raffaldini, T. (1988). The use of situation tests as measures of communicative ability. *Studies in Second Language Acquisition, 10,* 197–216.

Ravitch, D. (2003). *The language police: How pressure groups restrict what students learn.* New York: Knopf.

Rodabaugh, R. C. (1996). Institutional commitment to fairness in college teaching. In L. Fisch (Ed.), *Ethical dimensions of college and university teaching* (pp. 37–45). San Francisco: Jossey-Bass.

Rodriguez, M. C. (2003). Construct equivalence of multiple choice and constructed response items: A random effects synthesis of correlations. *Journal of Educational Measurement, 40*(2), 163–184.

Sawaki, Y., Quinlan, T., & Lee, Y. (2013). Understanding learner strengths and weaknesses: Assessing performance on an integrated writing task. *Language Assessment Quarterly, 10,* 73–95.

Scarino, A. (2013). Language assessment literacy as self-awareness: Understanding the role of interpretation in assessment and in teacher learning, *Language Testing, 30,* 309–327.

Schafer, J. (1981). The linguistic analysis of spoken and written texts. In B. Kroll & R. Vann (Eds.), *Exploring speaking-writing relationships: Connections and contrasts* (pp. 1–31). Urbana, IL: National Council of Teachers of English.

Scientists say global warming is undeniable. *Reuters.* Retrieved from www.abc.net.au/news/newsitems/200502/s1306233.html

Shavelson, R. J., Young, D. B., Ayala, C. C., Brandon, P. R., Furtak, E. M., Ruiz-Primo, M. A., & Yin, Y. (2008). On the impact of curriculum-embedded formative assessment on learning: A collaboration between curriculum and assessment developers, *Applied Measurement in Education, 21,* 295–314.

Shepard, L. A. (2000). *The role of classroom assessment in teaching and learning.* Los Angeles: National Center for Research on Evaluation, Standards, and Student Testing

Shohamy, E. (2000). Fairness in language testing. In A. Kunnan (Ed.), *Fairness and validation in language assessment* (pp. 15–19). Cambridge, U.K.: Cambridge University Press.

Shohamy, E. (2001). *The power of tests: A crucial perspective on the uses of language tests.* Essex, U.K.: Pearson Education.

Shohamy, E. (2007). The power of language tests, the power of the English language, and the role of ELT. In J. Cummins & C. Davison (Eds.), *International handbook of English language teaching* (pp. 521–531). New York: Springer.

Smith, M. L. (1991). Put to the test: The effects of external testing on teachers. *Educational Researcher, 20*(5), 8–11.

Stiggins, R. J. (2005). From formative assessment to assessment for learning: A path to success in standards-based schools. *Phi Delta Kappan, 87*(4), 324–328.

Stobart, G. (2005). Fairness in multicultural assessment systems. *Assessment in Education, 12*(3), 275–287.

Takala, S., & Kaftandjieva, F. (2000). Test fairness: A DIF analysis of an L2 vocabulary test. *Language Testing, 17*(3), 323–340.

Tate, W. (2001). Science education as a civil right: Urban schools and opportunity-to-learn considerations. *Journal of Research in Science Teaching, 38,* 1015–1028.

Taylor, L. (2010). Developing assessment literacy. *Annual Review of Applied Linguistics, 29,* 21–36.

Taylor, L. (2013). Communicating the theory, practice, and principles of language testing to test stakeholders: Some reflections. *Language Testing 30,* 403–412.

TESOL. (2006). *TESOL Pre K–12 English language proficiency standards.* Alexandria, VA: TESOL International Association.

Turner, C. E. (2000). Listening to the voices of rating scale developers: Identifying salient features for second language performance assessment. *The Canadian Modern Language Journal, 56,* 555–580.

Turner, C. E., & Upshur, J. A. (1996.) Developing rating scales for the assessment of second language performance. *Australian Review of Applied Linguistics, 13,* 55–79.

Turner, C. E., & Upshur, J. A. (2002). Rating scales derived from student samples: Effects of the scale maker and the student sample on scale content and students' scores. *TESOL Quarterly, 36*(1), 49–70.

Wall, D. (1997). Impact and washback in language testing. In C. Clapham & D. Corson (Eds.), *Encyclopedia of language and education, Volume 7. Language testing and assessment* (pp. 291–302). Dordrecht, the Netherlands: Kluwer Academic Publishers.

Webb, N. L. (1997). *Alignment of science and mathematics standards and assessments in four states* (Research Monograph No. 18). Madison: University of Wisconsin National Institute for Science Education.

Weigle, S.C. (1994). Effects of training on raters of ESL compositions. *Language Testing, 11*(2), 197–223.

Weigle, S.C. (1998). Using FACETS to model rater training effects. *Language Testing, 15*(2), 264–288.

Weigle, S. (2004). Integrating reading and writing in a competency test for non-native speakers of English. *Assessing Writing, 9*, 27–55.

Whitley, B. E., Perkins, D.V., Balogh, D. W., Keith-Spiegel, P. & Wittig, A.F. (July/August 2000). Fairness in the classroom. *APS Observer, 13*(6), 24–27.

Winke, P., Gass, S., & Myford, C. (2013). Raters' L2 background as a potential source of bias in rating oral performance. *Language Testing, 30*, 231–251.

Xie, Q. (2013). Does test preparation work? Implications for score validity, *Language Assessment Quarterly, 10*(2), 196–218.

Zhang, Y., & Elder, C. (2011). Judgments of oral proficiency by non-native and native English speaking teacher raters: Competing or complementary constructs? *Language Testing, 28*, 31–50.

Zieky, M. (2006). Fairness review in assessment. In S. Downing & T. Haladyna (Eds.), *Handbook of test development* (pp. 359–376). Mahwah, NJ: Lawrence Erlbaum.

Index

Don't Myth a Volume

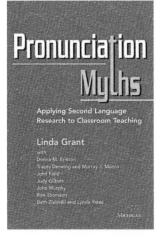

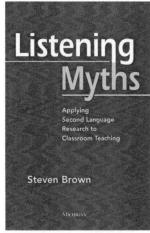

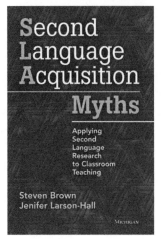

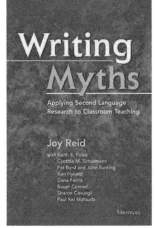

More Myths books planned for 2016